"Gary Haugen's splendidly written
book is a time bomb.
Read it prayerfully and seriously,
and sooner or later the combined chemistry
of his riveting presentation
of both planetary injustices and the imperatives
of Scripture will explode within you
and catapult you out in new ways
to our wounded world.
I predict that reading the book
and doing nothing about it
will be impossible."

MICHAEL CASSIDY
*founder and international team leader,
African Enterprise*

GOOD NEWS
ABOUT
INJUSTICE

A WITNESS OF COURAGE
IN A HURTING WORLD

GARY A. HAUGEN

InterVarsity Press
Downers Grove, Illinois, USA
Leicester, England

InterVarsity Press
P.O. Box 1400, Downers Grove, IL 60515, USA
World Wide Web: www.ivpress.com
E-mail: mail@ivpress.com

Inter-Varsity Press
38 De Montfort Street, Leicester LE1 7GP, England

InterVarsity Press®, U.S.A., is the book-publishing division of InterVarsity Christian Fellowship/USA®, a student movement active on campus at hundreds of universities, colleges and schools of nursing in the United States of America, and a member movement of the International Fellowship of Evangelical Students. For information about local and regional activities, write Public Relations Dept., InterVarsity Christian Fellowship/USA, 6400 Schroeder Rd., P.O. Box 7895, Madison, WI 53707-7895.

Inter-Varsity Press, England, is the book-publishing division of the Universities and Colleges Christian Fellowship (formerly the Inter-Varsity Fellowship), a student movement linking Christian Unions in universities and colleges throughout the United Kingdom and the Republic of Ireland, and a member movement of the International Fellowship of Evangelical Students. For information about local and national activities write to UCCF, 38 De Montfort Street, Leicester LE1 7GP.

Cover illustration: Tom Nelson/Tony Stone Images

USA ISBN 0-8308-2224-0
UK ISBN 0-85111-598-5

Printed in the United States of America ∞

Library of Congress Cataloging-in-Publication Data
Haugen, Gary A.
   Good news about injustice: a witness of courage in a hurting
world/Gary A. Haugen.
      p.   cm.
   Includes bibliographical references.
   ISBN 0-8308-2224-0 (pbk.: alk. paper)
   1. Christianity and justice.   I. Title.
BR115.J8H38   1999
   241',622—dc21
                                                                        99-17480
                                                                           CIP

British Library Cataloguing in Publication Data
A catalogue record for this book is available from the British Library.

20	19	18	17	16	15	14	13	12	11	10	9	8	7	6		
15	14	13	12	11	10	09	08	07	06	05	04	03	02	01	00	

For my father and mother

Foreword

Gary Haugen's book is a powerful combination of narrative and Scripture, of dramatic storytelling and biblical reflection, of human injustice and the justice of God.

One moment we are in the Rwandan killing fields, watching with mute horror the genocide of Tutsis, or in the red-light district of a large Asian city, whose brothels hold young children captive, while the next moment we are deep in Scripture, exploring the character and the will of God. And the interaction between these two perspectives continues throughout the book.

On the one hand, we are introduced to injustice, which always involves the abuse of power, and to the wide range of its victims. We are confronted not only with the cruelties of bonded labor, enforced prostitution, rape, torture, lynching and the misappropriation of land but also with the frequent failures of the law to bring the perpetrators to justice because they are protected by the establishment.

On the other hand, we are confronted in Scripture by the true and living God, who loves justice and hates injustice, whose anger is roused by evil and rests on evildoers, and who is moved with compassion toward all those who suffer.

What this book obliges us to do is to ask ourselves some basic and uncomfortable questions that living in a comfortable culture may never have allowed us to ask before.

First, what sort of God do we believe in? Is he concerned exclusively with individual salvation? Or does he have a social conscience? Is he (in Dr. Carl Henry's memorable phrase) "the God of justice and of justification"? How is it that so many of us staunch evangelical people have never seen, let alone faced, the barrage of biblical texts about justice? Why are we often guilty of selective indignation?

Second, what sort of a creature do we think a human being is? Have we ever considered the unique value and dignity of human beings, made in the image of God, so that abuse, torture, rape and grinding poverty, which dehumanize human beings, are also an insult to the God who made them?

Third, what sort of a person do we think Jesus Christ is? Have we ever seen him as described in John 11, where first he "snorted" with anger (v. 33, literally) in the face of death (an intrusion into God's good world) and then "wept" (v. 35) over the bereaved? If only we could be like Jesus, indignant toward evil and compassionate toward its victims!

Fourth, what sort of a community do we think the church is meant to be? Is it not often indistinguishable from the world because it accommodates itself to the prevailing culture of injustice and indifference? Is it not intended rather to penetrate the world like salt and light and so to change it, as salt hinders bacterial decay and light disperses darkness?

To ask ourselves these questions honestly—about God, Christ, human beings and the church—and to answer them biblically, as Gary Haugen does, is to expose ourselves to radical challenge and change.

The book does not leave us in suspense or with the doubts, the cynicism, even the despair which the world's monumental evil provokes in many Christian people. Instead, we are given solid grounds for hope. We are reminded of God's character, of his purpose to work through his people and of some of the heroic social reformers of the past. We are not given utopian visions of a perfect society, but we are encouraged to expect some substantial success both in defending human rights and in bringing to justice those who violate them. Gary Haugen outlines practical ways in which his International Justice Mission has been at work since 1994 and in which members of the body of Christ can contribute their distinctive gifts and specialist ministries.

I heartily commend this book. It is well researched and well written. Its author faces the unpleasant realities of our fallen world and responds to them with a biblically developed mind and conscience. He has the sharp eye of a lawyer and the sensitive spirit of an authentic disciple of Jesus Christ. He pulls no punches. We need to learn from him, to know what he knows, to see (at least in our imagination) what he sees and to feel what he feels.

I defy anybody to emerge from exposure to this book unscathed. In fact, my advice to would-be readers is "Don't! Leave the book alone!"—unless you are willing to be shocked, challenged, persuaded and transformed.

John Stott

Preface

As the father of four small children I find myself thinking more and more about the core gift I would like to give them to take into the world. I don't actually know the degree to which this gift is mine to give, but if I had one essential provision to grant as they were going out our door, I think I know what it would be. More and more I pray that our children might leave our home as men and women of courage. As C. S. Lewis wrote,

> Courage is not simply *one* of the virtues, but the form of every virtue at the testing point, which means, at the point of highest reality. A chastity or honesty or mercy which yields to danger will be chaste or honest or merciful only on conditions. Pilate was merciful till it became risky.[1]

Courage, however, is an odd gift because it's one we rarely think we'll want or need. It's like trying to get my preschoolers to put on their coats when there is no hint of winter's bitter cold inside our toasty home. Squirming and objecting, they doubt that it's as cold as all that outside, and more to the point they're not sure they even want to be going out.

Similarly, as a North American Christian I am not all that eager to accept the gift of courage that my God extends to me. I'm not all that sure I want to go to the places where I'll need it—to the places where virtues become risky. Sometimes staying indoors feels risky enough.

But then Jesus gently lets me know that I'm not living with a domesticated God. His prodding sounds much like the appeal my wife and I give to our own children to get them out the door: "Mom and Dad are going outside. We'll help you with your coats if you want to come with us." Likewise, I hear Jesus calling, "I'm going outside to a world that needs me. I'll help you with the courage you'll need if you want to be with me."

This book is an attempt to articulate something of the courage and hope that God is yearning to bestow on those who want to follow Christ into a world that needs his love. But it is the courage to extend the love of Jesus to a particular category of persons: the men, women and children who are victimized by the abuse of power.

As Christians we have learned much about sharing the love of Christ with people all over the world who have never heard the gospel. We continue to see the salvation message preached in the far corners of the earth and to see indigenous Christian churches vigorously extending Christ's kingdom on every continent. We have learned how to feed the hungry, heal the sick and shelter the homeless.

But there is one thing we haven't learned to do, even though God's Word repeatedly calls us to the task. We haven't learned how to rescue the oppressed. For the child held in forced prostitution, for the prisoner illegally detained and tortured, for the widow robbed of her land, for the child sold into slavery, we have almost no vision of how God could use us to bring tangible rescue. We don't know how to get the twelve-year-old girl *out* of the brothel, how to have the prisoner *set free,* how to have the widow's land *restored* to her or how to get the child slave *released* and the oppressors brought to justice.

It is perhaps more accurate to say that as people committed to the historic faith of Christianity, we have *forgotten* how to be such a witness of Christ's love, power and justice in the world. In generations past the great leaders of Christian revival in North America and Great Britain were consumed by a passion to declare the gospel and to manifest Christ's compassion and justice. But somewhere during the twentieth century some of us have simply stopped *believing* that God actually can use us to answer the prayers of children, women and families who suffer under the hand of abusive power or authority in their communities. We sit in the same paralysis of despair as those who don't even claim to know a Savior—and in some cases, we manifest even *less* hope.

In response this book has one simple message: it need not be this way. We can recover a witness of Christian courage in a world of injustice. We can rediscover our Maker's passions for the world and for justice—passions that may have grown unfamiliar to us. We can come to know the compassion of Jesus like never before as we go with him to look into the eyes of those who are in need of rescue. Moreover, we can be restored to the conviction that God is prepared to use *us* to "seek justice, rescue the oppressed, defend the orphan, plead for the widow" (Isaiah 1:17 NRSV).

Fundamentally, therefore, this book is offered as a testimonial, a reflection of what I have been learning about the world and about my Maker. And there has been much I've needed to learn. To be honest, few people could have grown up farther from the realities of injustice and oppression in our world than I did. I was raised in a wonderfully happy home. My loving family lived in an affluent suburb in a civil society—for which I am, frankly, enormously grateful. The realities of terror, oppression, abuse and injustice were kept far from my door. Not surprisingly, I came to understand God in ways that fit my experience. God seemed intensely interested in my life of personal piety and seemed most needed as a Savior from the only negative eventuality which I could not control—death. This is an oversimplification, of course, because I had the entire biblical revelation to draw on, but it serves to illustrate how relatively little I knew about a holy

God who spent his days weeping beside children in brothels, prisoners in pain or orphans in trauma—a God whose core hatred of injustice was rivaled only by his hatred of idolatry.

I knew little about the needs of the world or how God regarded such suffering. I knew even less about what those needs had to do with me or how I could make a difference. But eventually I left home. I lived in places where there was no escaping the raw realities of a world in rebellion against its Maker—apartheid in South Africa, guerilla war in the Philippines, genocide in Rwanda, to name a few. In these contexts I met followers of Jesus Christ who knew God more deeply, knew the Bible more thoroughly and lived life more courageously than I ever had. They didn't judge me or dismiss me for my limitations; they simply loved me and shared what they had learned, frequently the hard way, about the God of hope and power and joy. In time I found that I had developed some skills as an investigator and a lawyer that could actually be used to "seek justice, rescue the oppressed, defend the orphan, plead for the widow." I discovered that God was more than prepared to use his people as his instruments of truth and justice. He was prepared to work miracles through our modest offerings of compassion and obedience.

My personal introduction to the abuse of power in our world began shortly after my graduation from Harvard University. I spent a year working with South African church leaders on the National Initiative for Reconciliation during the brutal state of emergency of 1985-1986. After returning to the United States and studying law at the University of Chicago, my exposure to the pain of oppression in the world was deepened through my work for the Lawyers Committee for Human Rights, investigating the atrocities of abusive soldiers and police in the Philippines. Eventually I took a job as a trial attorney in the civil rights division of the United States Department of Justice. There I served on the police misconduct task force. While at the Department of Justice I was detailed to the United Nations in the fall of 1994 to serve as the director of the U.N. genocide investigation in Rwanda.

In the midst of these various overseas assignments I was struck by three simple but powerful facts. First, there were vast numbers of men, women and children in the world who were suffering. Second, within the communities where these abuses took place, Christian workers (missionaries, doctors, relief and development workers, and the like) knew a tremendous amount about these abuses yet felt helpless to do anything about them and had no idea where to turn for help. Finally, there were Christians who had the professional training, experience and resources to document these abuses and seek relief for victims—but there was no vehicle to bring their gifts and energy to bear on these needs.

In response to this need a number of Christian friends and colleagues came together to form the International Justice Mission in 1994. This organization makes available a corps of Christian public justice professionals (lawyers, criminal investigators, diplomats, government relations experts and the like) to serve global Christian workers when they encounter cases of abuse or oppression in their communities. The International Justice Mission documents the abuses and seeks relief for the victims either directly or in partnership with indigenous advocacy groups or through other international human rights organizations. Through the grace of God the International Justice Mission has been able to bring effective advocacy and relief to hundreds of victims of abuse throughout the world—girls released from forced prostitution, children rescued from illegal bonded servitude, prisoners released from illegal detention and abusive police brought to account, to name a few.

This then is the story of that journey, and my prayer will be answered if it conveys even a small measure of the hope and encouragement that the God of justice intends for his people. In expressing this prayer I hasten to add that this modest volume is not an exhaustive treatment of anything. It is not a thorough survey of injustice and human-rights abuses in the world, for many of the most severe may not even be mentioned. Sadly, there is just too much material to work with. Neither is this a full theological treatment of the character of the

God of justice, for, happily, there is too much biblical material to work with. My modest aspiration is not to stimulate reflection on sophisticated biblical arcana but on some of the most arrestingly blunt declarations of Scripture. Finally, I have not set out to write a complete manual on human-rights advocacy but merely to provide some concrete pictures of the practical difference Christians can make in rescuing the oppressed, and to offer starting principles for overcoming the forces of injustice.

This book is a simple introduction to three things: the injustice of our world, the character of our God, and the opportunity for God's people to make a difference. Part one opens with an overview of the reality of injustice, suggests how we can prepare spiritually to combat it and offers examples of how other Christians have tackled the task.

Since in the face of suffering we can easily be immobilized by despair, in part two I deal with four affirmations that God makes about justice, which offer us hope to get beyond that despair. In looking at God's character we can see how he feels about injustice and those who suffer under it. Part three provides some answers to the difficult questions injustice raises for us as Christians and some real-world tools for understanding how injustice works, investigating the deceptions of oppressors, intervening for victims and doing what each of us can, given our talents and resources, to rescue the oppressed.

It should be noted that for reasons of security and personal sensitivity, pseudonyms have been used to obscure the identities of some of the individuals whose stories are shared in this book.

In preparing this work I have been profoundly assisted by the research and editorial support of my colleagues at the International Justice Mission, particularly Jocelyn Penner, Leslie Grimes, Daryl Kreml, Kristin Romens, Lindsey Etheridge and Ryan Cobb. I am also grateful for the editorial assistance and encouragement of Gary Albert, Joan Albert and Ann Haugen Michael. While I was preparing the book, Sam Dimon, Art Gay, Clyde Taylor and Vera Shaw kindly and faithfully upheld me in prayer. I am very grateful for the personal encouragement of Dr. Luis Lugo and the financial support of the Pew Charitable Trusts. I have also been the beneficiary of much kindness and support from Hugh O. Maclellan Jr., Tom MacCallie and Daryl Heald. I and the International Justice Mission staff would also like to express our thanks to the directors and staff of the Library of Congress and the library of the Virginia Theological Seminary. I am also very thankful for the encouragement and support of Dr. Steve Hayner, president of InterVarsity Christian Fellowship, and for the commitment and faith of InterVarsity Press in publishing this work.

As many will readily appreciate, I am deeply humbled by the kind encouragement and collaboration of the Reverend John Stott, and for the kindness extended by his assistant John Yates III.

My deepest gratitude goes to my wife, Jan. Words are too poor to express the measure of love and joy you have extended to me in your companionship throughout this project and the larger journey. My joy has been walking closely together in thought, in words, in heart, in laughter and in faith. You have been that sheltering tree of grace from which courage proceeds. You are abiding faith, hope and love.

Finally, whatever may be the strengths or weaknesses of this work, these words will be of little note and short remembrance in the scope of God's grace and work in our world. What will last is the Word of God and his work of love among us.

But whatever was to my profit I now consider loss for the sake of Christ. What is more, I consider everything a loss compared to the surpassing greatness of knowing Christ Jesus my Lord, for whose sake I have lost all things. I consider them rubbish, that I may gain Christ and be found in him, not having a righteousness of my own that comes from the law, but that which is through faith in Christ—the righteousness that comes from God and is by faith. (Philippians 3:7-9)

Part 1

Taking Up the Challenge

One

The Rage in Rwanda

A Suburban Christian Confronts Genocide

I REMEMBER LOOKING UP FROM MY NEWSPAPER DURING MY BUS ride to work one morning in the fall of 1994 and finding everything oddly in place. The AT4 bus was proceeding apace at 8:17 a.m. in the car-pool zone. I was comfortably settled in my usual seat one row from the center double doors. My good-natured but nameless neighbors were sitting where they ought and respectively sleeping, reading or talking too loud, according to schedule. The low morning sun was where it should be, creating the glare that always forced me to look up from my paper at that point in the route. In that moment, pausing and looking around at all that American commuter normalcy, something inside me wanted to say, "Excuse me, friends, but did you know that less than forty-eight hours ago I was standing in the middle of several thousand corpses in a muddy mass grave in a tiny African country called Rwanda?"

Ascension: Coming Back from a Hell on Earth
The Scriptures do not tell us very much about Jesus' ascension, his

sudden transport from earth to heaven. But there have been moments
in my life when I wish they did. All we know is that he was standing
with his rather earthy friends on an earthen hill trying as ever to explain
something, when "he was taken up into heaven and he sat at the right
hand of God" (Mark 16:19). That is all there is to it: one minute earth,
the next minute heaven.

The very suddenness of it has always seemed to me something to
ponder. What was it like for Jesus, as a man, to be transported in an
instant from a horrifically fallen earth of darkness and death to a
heavenly country of light and life—to a city that "does not need the
sun or the moon to shine on it, for the glory of God gives it light"
(Revelation 21:23)? What sort of mental adjustment, if we may call it
that, was required to move so suddenly from the nightmarish world of
the cross—a world of betrayal and torture, of blood lust and wailing
women—to paradise? What was it like for the divine Man in heaven
to exchange in a moment the stench of death and his own encrusted
grave clothes for the very fragrance of life, a white robe, a golden sash
and a seat at the right hand of the throne of God—to be home at last
with his Father, where "there will be no more death or mourning or
crying or pain" (Revelation 21:4)?

These may be idle questions, but they have come to me with
particular force as I have struggled with the unreality of my own
ascension experiences—moments when I have been transported with
almost ethereal speed from a hell on earth to a heaven on earth. In a
matter of hours I have traveled from the slippery mud and corpses of
mass graves in Rwanda to my usual seat at the right hand of my
neighbor on our dependably boring and climate-controlled bus ride to
my office in Washington, D.C. I remember reclining on a comfortable
living-room couch, among friends and family in California, talking
about soaring real estate values in Orange County when only days
before I had been exhuming the remains of a woman raped and
butchered by soldiers in the Philippines. Similarly, I recall watching

from my train window as a low summer sun cast a Norman Rockwell glow across Little League fields in Connecticut when only days before I had been in a country where boys of a similar age but of a different color were being beaten like animals by the South African police.

I don't know whether Jesus experienced dreams while he was here on earth or whether he felt as if he had awakened from a particularly bad one when he found himself back in heaven after his ascension from the earth. But I have certainly felt that dreamlike separation from reality when I have returned from these hellish places around the world. In no time at all it begins to feel as if the nightmare I came from in Rwanda or the Philippines or South Africa has taken place not in another country but on another planet. Back home, it simply does not feel *real* anymore.

Thus my sudden urge to make that announcement about the Rwandan genocide to unsuspecting fellow bus commuters came not from a desire to shock them but from a desire to somehow affirm for myself the human reality and relevance of my own experience. Could it really be true, and could it really have anything to do with me, that in a period of about six weeks in the spring of 1994, about half a million defenseless women and children were hacked to death by their neighbors in the towns and villages of Rwanda?

I remember very well what *I* was doing in the spring of 1994. I was trying to assemble cribs for twin girls who were coming into our home, ready or not. I was trying to match wits, and losing, with the class clown in my sixth-grade boys' Sunday-school class. I was seeking every advantage, and losing, in my effort to trade in our Honda Civic for a Taurus station wagon. I was prevailing in my arguments in a trial in federal court in Alabama, enjoying an occasional jog along the Potomac River in Washington, D.C., and denying that I had ever watched *Melrose Place* on TV.

Like most Americans in the spring of 1994, I was also starting to see horrible stories in the newspapers about some kind of "tribal

warfare" in an African country I had never heard much about. Then I
saw pictures on the evening news of bloated bodies floating down a
river and heard commentators talking about genocide. Apparently
thousands, maybe even millions, of Tutsis were being slaughtered by
their Hutu compatriots in a genocidal hysteria sweeping across
Rwanda. But like most of the great ugliness transmitted by TV across
the world and into my living room, the terror in Rwanda just did not
seem real. It seemed *true*, but not real—not to me. I did not dispute
the accuracy of the reports, but they might as well have been pictures
from Sojourner on Mars or reports about people who lived in ancient
Rome or statistics about how many bizillion other solar systems are
in the Milky Way—all true enough, but not real. Not real like my kids
when they are sick, not real like my job when I am behind in my work,
not real like my neighbors when one of them has been in a car accident,
not even real like my Midwestern compatriots when they have been
flooded out of their homes.

Meeting the Truth in Rwanda

But then in the fall of 1994 I went to Rwanda. Only forty-eight hours
before taking my seat on the AT4 commuter bus, I had been in Kibuye,
Rwanda, a beautiful town sprawling on the banks of Lake Kivu and
clinging to the green highlands of eastern Rwanda—and a horrible
town—where thousands of Tutsis (mostly women and children) were
hacked and beaten to death by their Hutu neighbors over a period of
several days. I was in Kibuye directing the U.N.'s genocide investigation in the country, on loan to the United Nations from the U.S.
Department of Justice. My job was to march down a list of mass grave
and massacre sites provided by U.N. military intelligence and deploy
our international investigative teams to gather preliminary evidence
against the perpetrators. The evidence would eventually be turned over
to the International Criminal Tribunal for Rwanda, which was just
being established to bring the murderers to justice. There in Kibuye,

and in scores of other towns and villages across the country, the nightmare became real for me.

Kibuye was my last mass grave site before I was to head back home to America. One of my twin infant daughters had been stricken with meningitis, and while our worst fears had passed and she was on the mend, it was time for me to return to my family. For this final project in Kibuye I brought four other members of my U.N. investigative team: Luc, a jovial, bear-sized criminal lawyer from French Canada; Jim, a delightfully wry police officer from Northern Ireland; Thaddi, a Rwandan school teacher who served as interpreter; and Nehemiah, our U.N. military officer from Zimbabwe who mostly missed his family back home. We arrived in Kibuye after a jarring, five-hour, four-wheel-drive journey from our headquarters in Kigali.

Once we arrived, the most dangerous part of our assignment was over. Though low-level civil war still claimed the country, land mines peppered the fields and bandits roamed the land, the greatest danger was simply traveling on the roads. Narrow, mud-washed trails over sheer mountain cliffs wound their way over the eastern highlands and delivered us to the banks of Lake Kivu—one of the great, deep-blue lakes of Africa—separating Rwanda from Zaire. Of course, the breathtaking beauty of the lake and its lush tropical shores were marred by human horror, for we knew that many corpses found their way to the placid waters during the genocide only a few months before.

Murder investigations generally begin where the bodies are, and as we arrived in Kibuye, I knew this meant that we would be heading for the biggest church in town—the Catholic cathedral and the adjoining Home St. Jeans, a complex of residential and educational buildings. The large, rough-hewn stone cathedral stood sturdy and squat on a peninsula over the lake. The stone and concrete interior had been scrubbed out, but as we stepped inside, we found the lingering, overpowering essence that could not be cleansed from the stones—the stifling, unnatural odor of a mass sepulcher. For within these walls and on this floor, hundreds of defenseless children, mothers, brothers and grandmothers had been hacked and clubbed to death in a murderous binge of torture and slaughter just months ago. Now the cathedral was empty, except for a lone, deranged man in rags, who had made the empty hall his home and was seen spending hours on his knees mumbling before the altar.

Gathering All the Facts
Our task in the coming days was to conduct an investigative site survey, locate survivors and other witnesses and begin to account for the bodies. The story that emerged was a familiar one. On April 6, 1994, the president of Rwanda was killed in a mysterious plane crash in Kigali, the capital city. Almost immediately extremist Hutu factions within the government and the military joined with extremist Hutu paramilitary groups across the country to incite a murderous hysteria against Tutsis and moderate Hutu. The quasi-ethnic divisions between Hutu and Tutsis in Rwanda had been highly politicized over the years, with each side viewing the struggle as a zero sum game between governance and extinction. Claiming that Tutsis had killed their president and were now coming to slaughter all Hutu, these fanatical Hutu leaders used government military forces, citizen militia and local mobs to start hunting down and killing the Tutsis in their communities. In the days following the plane crash, Tutsis in and around Kibuye began to hear of prominent members of their community being dragged from their homes and murdered. Disheveled Tutsi corpses began to appear in the streets.

By April 17 the violence and hysteria had reached a full boil in Kibuye. Seeking safety in numbers and following the orders of the provincial governor and the mayor, hundreds of Tutsi men, women and children huddled together at the cathedral and the Home St. Jeans complex. During times of ethnic conflict in years past, many Tutsi had found sanctuary within the sacred walls of churches across the country. So as the fever of violence escalated in Kibuye and across Rwanda, the churches became packed to the rafters with thousands of trembling women and children seeking refuge. For the hundreds huddled in the Kibuye cathedral, however, there would be no refuge, only a lure, a trap and a grave.

On that day in April the provincial governor and mayor, who had ordered all Tutsi to the cathedral (ostensibly for their safety), ordered that the complex be surrounded. Eventually a force assembled from members of the Gendarmeri Nationale (the national police), the local police from the commune, Interhamwe (the extremist Hutu militia group) and an armed mob of local civilians. The governor then unleashed this combined army upon the defenseless people.

Working largely with machetes, metal rods, spears and wooden clubs with nails partially embedded at the head, the mob cut the Tutsis—men, women and children—down by the hundreds and bludgeoned them to death.

In the days that followed, the Gendarmerie Nationale, Interhamwe and armed civilians hunted down and killed any survivors they could find. One survivor we interviewed, a young father of three children, said that he had seen his entire family murdered around him. He survived, but for three days he crawled among the dead on the cathedral floor, wounded and desperately thirsty. He said he nearly smothered a surviving child from another family who wanted to cry out when the murderers returned to beat more survivors to death.

When the orgy of murder had exhausted itself, the killers moved on to the Kibuye stadium where an even larger group of frightened Tutsis had gathered for protection. The brick-walled stadium sat between the town's main road and a steep hill made of the same red clay. By April 18 the police, Interhamwe militia and local mob had surrounded the stadium and were killing anyone trying to escape. Huddled by the thousands within the stadium walls and between the brick grandstand and the thick green grass in the oval, the Tutsi men, women and children cried out for rescue and for mercy but found none. According to reports it was once again the provincial governor, Clement Kayishema, who raised his pistol to the air and fired off the signal to attack.

With a rush the blood-lusting mob waded into the sea of screaming and scrambling villagers. All day the mob hacked and blasted its way through its Tutsi neighbors—most deaths coming ultimately with a massive machete blow to the head. The exhausting task could not be completed in a single day, however, so with the police and militia sealing off the stadium during the night, the attackers took their evening rest, returning the next morning for another full day of mass murder. Thus by the end of the next day the stadium, like the cathedral, was silent with death and heaps of broken bodies.

Beyond the Facts: Artifacts and Survivors Tell Their Stories
By the time I arrived in Kibuye to direct the U.N. military in digging up the two mass graves where all these broken bodies had eventually been flung, it was easy to think of them as exactly that: nameless, faceless, decaying and disconnecting body parts. I had a job to do—to turn over enough of the mass grave at the cathedral and the stadium to corroborate the testimony of our witnesses, and then to move on. It was a filthy, stinking job, but it had to be done. We were busy, and it simply did not pay to think very hard about any particular story represented by any particular set of the remains I was now rearranging for forensic photographs. It had not seemed worth thinking too much about months ago when I saw the pictures at home on TV of Tutsi bodies floating down a river somewhere in Africa. Now that those same anonymous corpses were at my feet, it still felt more comfortable to think of them as a tragic mass rather than as anything like the individual people that I knew and cared about back home.

But at Kibuye, as at every massacre site in Rwanda, a painful glimpse of the truth always came through. This was not an undifferentiated mass of lifeless clods on the inevitable dust heap of a fallen world. In truth each body, now dull and limp in the mud, was actually a unique bearer of the very image of God, a unique creation of the divine Maker, individually knit within a mother's womb by the Lord of the universe. For as difficult as it was to imagine, each crumpled mortal frame had indeed come from a mother, one single mother who somewhere in time had wept tears of joy and aspiration over her precious child—a child endowed with the mysterious spark of Adam and an immortal soul. We would never number all the mother's children in these mass graves, but their Father in heaven had numbered even the very hairs of their heads.

It made my job infinitely more difficult to look at the dead this way, but day after day, pieces of the truth would work their way into my heart. These mass graves might appear as vague, dark images of generalized evil in an unjust world, but in truth they were an intimate family portrait with a story for every face—each member of the human family having lived and died as one individual at a time.

These stories gradually emerged from the artifacts and survivors. Every massacre site had stories to tell from what was left behind. Tutsis had fled their homes from miles around to seek safety in these churches, stadiums and schools. Many brought with them their most cherished personal possessions, and it was these items that now testified to their humanity in a way that their lifeless forms could not. Of course, anything of value had long been stripped away, leaving only those things that people clutch in death but robbers do not steal—pictures from a wedding day, a French Bible with a loving inscription, a small calendar with pictures of faraway places.

And then there were the stacks of government-issued, mandatory identity cards. In sites where we had only skeletal remains, the identity cards said everything that needed saying. Each card featured a fading black-and-white photograph, a picture of just one person, with a face different from all the rest, looking tired, proud, embarrassed or caught off guard. And each bore a check in the box next to the word *Tutsi*. Despite the mind-numbing scale of the genocide, these little pale-green cards spoke the truth about injustice in the world. Just as with famine, despite appearances, people really do die one person at a time.

Yet it was still hard for me to connect myself to these people—these people who were no more, people I never knew, people who must be so different from me and mine. It certainly made my work more tolerable to view them this way.

In the end it wasn't the remaining artifacts but the survivors in Rwanda who took me across a mysterious bridge that allowed me to behold the same human heart, eyes and hands of these, my departed neighbors.

The Truth of Injustice Becomes Personal and Real

Some time ago I stopped being surprised by the existence of survivors from such massacres. As I have learned, human beings are strangely easy, and strangely hard, to kill. And each survivor has a miraculous and horrible tale to tell.

I once took testimony from a woman in the Philippines who had been shot in the torso several times by a high-powered firearm at short range. She had the scars to show for it. This woman, called Rose, and seventeen other members of her little village in Northern Luzon had been rounded up by angry soldiers and gunned down in the middle of a rice paddy. She was pregnant at the time of the massacre, and she and the baby were in good health when I met them more than a year after the incident. She was, in fact, a charming young woman— engaging, funny, clever—who had a certain guarded melancholy, no doubt, but no despair. She was a hard-working, generous mother and neighbor. She cared for many, and many cared for her. The resilient spark in her eyes and the life in her smile made one wonder how brilliant that sparkle must have been before her nightmare with the Philippine Army.

Nevertheless, had one of the bullets taken even a slightly different course through her abdomen, I would have never known of Rose. I would have only known of eighteen, rather than seventeen, lifeless victims of an ugly, dirty war in the Philippines. Rose told the truth about a mass grave and about massive injustice in our world, and so did the survivors I met in Rwanda.

Two little girls in Kibuye, with shy smiles of perfect and brilliantly white teeth, showed us the thick, pink scars across the neck of one and across the head of the other. They were being interviewed by Luc and Thaddi in a dilapidated schoolroom when Jim and I joined them after a very long day at the mass grave near the stadium.

I had been picking through human garbage almost all day. I was exhausted, sunburned and dirty. Jim and I pulled up one of the frail, narrow school benches in the back of the room and watched the conversation between Luc, Thaddi and the little girls. They told stories about where they lived, the animals they liked, the families they used to have and the neighbors who were caring for them now. Through it all they were the picture of courage, sadness and sweetness. At the end of the interview they were dismissed and left the room tugging each other close with whispers. Luc finished his notes with Thaddi.

As Jim and I waited, I had too much time to think. I was pierced again with the true identity of the rubbish I had been forced to wallow in all day. These two little girls—they were the rubbish. Though "fearfully and wonderfully made" (like my own two little girls at home), the awfulness of evil, the remoteness of Rwanda and the lifelessness of death had conspired to very nearly rob these little ones of their human face. I found myself trying to blink back the wave of emotion and the tears in my eyes. I stared hard at the smooth concrete floor and started quietly whistling through my teeth.

After a moment, I heard my own idle tune: "Jesus loves me / This I know / For the Bible tells me so / Little ones to him belong / They are weak / But he is strong." In another moment, I heard Jim whistling a soft harmony behind me. Apparently he too had been to Sunday school. We sat waiting a bit longer for Luc to finish, walked back to the truck and rode silently home to our base camp. Jim and I never spoke of the moment to one another.

Seeking Justice: God's Compassion, Commandment and Commission

These were tough moments for me, but there was no longer any question about what this horrible injustice in Rwanda had to do with me, a suburban American lawyer who rode a bus to work during the week and taught sixth-grade Sunday school on the weekend. It had everything to do with me because of what my God loves and what my God hates. To quote another Sunday-school chorus: "Jesus loves the little children / *All* the children of the world / Red and yellow, black and white / They are precious in his sight." Rwanda might seem far away, and these Rwandan children might seem different from my own, but I do not know anything about my God or the truth of my own childish choruses if I do not understand that, truly, "red and yellow, black and white, they are precious in his sight."

Moreover, this has everything to do with me because God hates injustice. "The LORD examines the righteous, but the wicked and those who love violence his soul hates. . . . For the LORD is righteous, he loves justice" (Psalm 11:5, 7). The Bible says that when officials are acting like "wolves tearing their prey, shedding blood, destroying lives for dishonest gain," the Lord looks for someone to "stand in the breach," to "intervene" and to "seek justice" (Isaiah 1:17; 59:15-16; Ezekiel 22:25, 27, 30 NRSV). By the time I arrived in Kibuye, I was much too late to stop the killing. I couldn't bring the dead back to life or back to their families. But it matters to God whether the evildoers are brought to justice:

[The wicked man] lies in wait near the villages;

from ambush he murders the innocent,
watching in secret for his victims.
He lies in wait like a lion in cover;
he lies in wait to catch the helpless;
he catches the helpless and drags them off in his net.
His victims are crushed, they collapse;
they fall under his strength.
He says to himself, "God has forgotten;
he covers his face and never sees."
Arise, LORD! Lift up your hand, O God.
Do not forget the helpless.
Why does the wicked man revile God?
Why does he say to himself,
"He won't call me to account"?
But you, O God, do see trouble and grief;
you consider it to take it in hand.
The victim commits himself to you;
you are the helper of the fatherless.
Break the arm of the wicked and evil man;
call him to account for his wickedness
that would not be found out. (Psalm 10:8-15)

It matters to me, therefore, that the leaders of the Kibuye massacre (the governor, the mayor and their accomplices) have been captured and indicted by the International Criminal Tribunal for Rwanda. As I write, they are being "called to account." The prosecution has presented closing arguments and is recommending four terms of life imprisonment on counts of genocide and crimes against humanity, and a minimum of forty additional years on violations of the Geneva Convention. This is partly through the testimony of survivors and witnesses that we interviewed inside that little schoolroom—including those two little orphans with shy smiles of perfect teeth. Of course, convicting the war criminals of Kibuye ultimately cannot bring true justice and healing to Rwanda or to those little girls. Nor can it or any other human mechanism promise ultimate peace and salvation for the human race. But by calling these men to account we can hope that the next generation of wicked "princes" will think twice about perpetrating such abuses, and the dead will not be mocked by impunity for their murderers.

In any case, seeking justice is a straightforward command of God for his people and part of Christ's prayer that his Father's will be done "on earth as it is in heaven" (Matthew 5:10). At least for me as a Christian, it is part of my testimony about the character of the God I love: "You hear O LORD, the desire of the afflicted; you encourage them, and you listen to their cry, defending the fatherless and the oppressed, in order that man, who is of the earth, may terrify no more" (Psalm 10:17-18).

The great miracle and mystery of God is that he calls me and you to be a part of what he is doing in history. He could, of course, with no help from us proclaim the gospel of Jesus Christ with lifeless stones, feed the entire world with five loaves and two fish, heal the sick with the hem of his garment and release all the oppressed with his angels. Instead God has chosen us—missionaries, agricultural engineers, doctors, lawyers, lawmakers, diplomats and all those who support, encourage and pray for them—to be his hands in doing those things in the world that are important to him.

When Christ ascended into heaven, he left behind only two things for the fulfillment of all his aspirations for the world: his Spirit and his followers. With the Holy Spirit we have been commissioned to demonstrate Christ's love for all the world: to disciple the nations, to feed the hungry, to clothe the naked, to heal the broken and even to rescue the oppressed. When we sing that all children are "precious in his sight," we must not forget that he, of whom we sing, has declared himself to be the God of justice. Scripture describes the one who follows God: "He will deliver the needy who cry out, the afflicted who have no one to help. He will take pity on the weak and the needy and save the needy from death. He will rescue them from oppression and violence, for *precious is their blood in his sight"* (Psalm 72:12-14).

The Scriptures promise that "a scepter of justice will be the scepter of [God's] kingdom" (Psalm 45:6). And while the kingdom of God will be complete only in the coming of Christ, today our great joy and privilege is to work as colaborers with the Creator in extending his kingdom over one more life, one more family, one more neighborhood, one more community. The people of God will find in Christ the compassion and courage to engage the call to justice, for we know God *promises* that we who do not "become weary in doing good . . . will reap a harvest if we do not give up" (Galatians 6:9).

When We See Injustice, We Have a Choice

Many who lack faith will shrink away from the distant, dark world of injustice. Still others will water down the Word and imagine that they can love God without loving their brother, or wanting to "justify" themselves, they will invent elaborate quibbles with Jesus about who is and is not their neighbor (Luke 10:25-37; 1 John 3:10, 16-18). To these the Lord says: "When you stretch out your hands, I will hide my eyes from you; even though you make many prayers, I will not listen. . . . Learn to do good; seek justice, rescue the oppressed, defend the orphan, plead for the widow" (Isaiah 1:15-17 NRSV).

Others, by contrast, recognizing the voice of their Good Shepherd will respond with joy: "Here I am. Send me!" (Isaiah 6:8). They will embrace the orphans and widows of the world, as their Savior did. With the hurting, the oppressed and the abused in mind, these people will come to the Master with their meager offering, their widow's mite, their inadequate loaves and fishes and simply say, "Jesus, can you do anything with these?" And while the men "close" to Jesus will scoff, "How far will they go among so many?" Jesus himself will say, "Bring them here to me" (Matthew 14:18; John 6:9).

To be witnesses to the love of Christ in such a large, brutally unjust world seems overwhelming and beyond our calling. Even so, Jesus speaks to us. When he departed this earth for heaven—so suddenly, so mysteriously—he left much unexplained. But he wanted us to know one thing: we will receive from him power, the power to be his witnesses in word and deed "to the ends of the earth" (Acts 1:8-9).

For the little Filipino girl abducted into prostitution, for the Pakistani boy chained to a weaving loom, for the Latin American widow pushed off her land and even for the African father rotting in his prison cell without a charge or a trial, we share Christ's saving love on the cross and the servant love of our hands. As it was in days of old, "it will be a sign and witness to the LORD Almighty in the land of Egypt. When they cry out to the LORD because of their oppressors, he will send them a savior and defender, and he will rescue them" (Isaiah 19:20).

"Here I am, Lord. Send me!"

Two

Preparing the Mind & Spirit Through Scripture

ANYONE WHO HAS SPENT TIME WITH INFANTS KNOWS WHAT amazing machines of tireless learning and curiosity they are. We can also see that during an early stage of development, an infant has no capacity to maintain interest in anything that is not immediately before its eyes. When a brightly colored ball or rattle is held up before babies, their attention is riveted on it. Their eyes seize on the new item with urgent curiosity. They display an almost compulsive urge to touch it, feel it, embrace it. But move the toy out of sight and infants lose all interest. They do not look for it. They do not try to bring back the hand that took the toy away. They do not express any disappointment that the toy is no longer there to explore. As far as child psychologists are able to discern, to babies the toy ceases to exist the very moment it is removed from sight. They have not yet developed the mental capacity for *object permanence,* that is, the understanding that objects exist even when they are out of sight. It is truly a case of out of sight, out of mind.

I must confess that this is very much the way my mind often works when it comes to maintaining an interest in the reality of injustice in our world. I read about innocent people being slaughtered in Rwanda on page A1 of the *Washington Post,* and I am appalled. But my mind moves on to other things with amazing speed and thoroughness when I read on page D15 that the movie my wife and I were hoping to see actually starts a half hour earlier than we thought. When I read about the way abandoned orphan girls in China are tied to their bed rails and left to starve and die in state-run orphanages, I am very nearly moved to tears. But a year later when a conversation with a friend reminds me of the article, I realize that I have not shed a tear, uttered a prayer or even given it thought since the day I put down that newspaper article. I can move from torture on the evening news to touchdowns on Monday Night Football with almost the same mental and emotional ease as my channel changer.

Of course, much of this is perfectly natural and probably healthy. I do not aspire to be someone with a psychotic fixation on evil and human suffering. It is a poorly lived life that cannot experience joy, peace, laughter, beauty and mirth despite all the oppression and injustice that mars the goodness of God's creation. If the evening news or the morning paper keeps me from taking my wife to a movie, from laughing at my three-year-old daughter's stories or from enjoying the exhilaration of a bike ride on a crisp fall day, then something is surely out of balance.

But we *can* grow into a more mature way of engaging the reality of injustice in our world if we take just two steps: (1) We can develop a compassion for the people suffering injustice by looking through the eyes of missionaries and other Christian workers who see this suffering firsthand, and (2) we can prepare ourselves to help people by looking at them through God's eyes, that is, through his Word.

The First Step: Cultivating a Compassionate Awareness
Perhaps a next step in our development as children of God is a capacity

for *compassion permanence*—a courageous and generous capacity to remember the needs of an unjust world even when they are out of our immediate sight. Not content with the infant's out-of-sight, out-of-mind approach, God calls us to a grown-up capacity to engage a world of oppression with our heart and mind, even though (thankfully) it is not always before our eyes.

Christians, of course, are meant to be particularly gifted in sustaining a commitment to what is true and important though unseen. The very essence of faith, we are told, is "the conviction of things unseen" (Hebrews 1:11). Therefore, we who are only rarely exposed first- or secondhand to the truth about those who suffer injustice in our world are taught in Scripture to "remember" what we know, even after it leaves our site or experience. "Remember those in prison as if you were their fellow prisoners, and those who are mistreated as if you yourselves were suffering" (Hebrews 13:3). We are to recall the plight of the poor and the imprisoned (Galatians 2:10; Colossians 4:18). Precisely because it is not our first and natural inclination, we are called to a conscious effort of reserving a space in our thought life for those who suffer abuse and oppression in our world.

Admittedly, this calling strikes me as burdensome. On any given day I am so busy trying to order the stress and vulnerability out of my own life that the notion of remembering a child prostitute in India, a torture victim in Indonesia or a child laborer in Honduras seems beyond the core of my Christian calling. But what is the core of my Christian calling? Every Christian who knows her Bible has a ready answer: to love God and to love our neighbor as ourselves (Matthew 22:37-40). Christ taught us that to love our neighbor was to treat people the way we would like to be treated (Luke 6:31). Accordingly, the call to remember the oppressed is couched in the logic of love: "Remember . . . those who are mistreated *as if you yourselves were suffering*." The Scriptures are confident that if we imagine we are the child prostitute, the torture victim, the child laborer, we would not want to be forgotten. Surely, it is God's job to remember *all* the victims of injustice in our world, but might there not be one child, one prisoner, one widow, one refugee that I can remember?

Seeing and listening to what the body of Christ sees and hears. For Christians living in a relatively affluent and orderly civil society, this act of remembering the injustice and abuse in the world is not an easy one. But it is not a new challenge either. In the third century St. Cyprian wrote to his friend in North Africa about the trouble he was having remembering the true nature of the world into which Christ had cast his disciples:

> This seems a cheerful world when I view it from this fair garden under the shadow of these vines. But if I climbed some great mountain and looked out over the wide lands, you know very well what I would see. Brigands on the high road, pirates on the seas, in the amphitheaters men murdered to please the applauding crowds, under all roofs misery and selfishness. It is really a bad world Donatus, an incredibly bad world.

To be honest, as an American suburban professional I pass most of my days with my family in the gentle shade of a very fair garden. We have our problems and stresses, but on most days, if we are not indulging our own self-pity or covetousness, the world we see seems cheerful indeed. I say that not as one who is unfamiliar with the injustice and oppression that persists in American communities. In fact, after a career as a trial attorney in the civil rights division of the U.S. Department of Justice, I imagine I have seen more than most— especially after my tour on the police-misconduct task force. One case I encountered in New Orleans, where two police officers raped a teenage runaway and dropped her back out on the streets, rivaled the brutality I have seen in almost any country. Even so, this girl did have a place to turn for justice, and those two police officers are now behind bars. Throughout the world, however, such incidents are repeated with impunity hundreds of times a day. Relative to what lies out in the world, ours is among the shadiest and fairest of gardens.

So to see the hurting world as God sees it, we need to go with St. Cyprian and look out over the wide lands of this incredibly bad world. And who better to help us do that than the countless Christian missionaries and service workers that we send out around the globe?

In 1996 the International Justice Mission asked nearly seventy evangelical ministries serving globally in missions and relief and development to be the church's eyes and ears in the world. These ministries support tens of thousands of Christian workers in more than a hundred countries. When asked in our survey, every single ministry indicated that they had workers serving in communities where people suffered injustice and abuse in circumstances where local authorities could not be relied on for relief. These seventy ministries named the following categories of injustices as the most widely observed:

☐ abusive child labor
☐ abusive police or military
☐ child pornography
☐ child prostitution
☐ corrupt seizure or extortion of land
☐ detention or disappearance without charge or trial
☐ extortion or withholding of wages
☐ forced adult/teenage prostitution
☐ forced migration
☐ genocide
☐ murder of street children
☐ organized political intimidation
☐ organized racial violence
☐ public justice corruption
☐ state, rebel or paramilitary terrorism
☐ state-supported discrimination or abuse of ethnic minorities

☐ state-sponsored religious persecution
☐ state-sponsored torture

Of course these are just words on a list. It takes stories from those Christian workers to give them meaning.

Child prostitution. One ministry that works with street children in Manila told me about the day they started to notice that some of the little girls with whom they had been working were disappearing from their ministry. These were little orphans and runaways between the ages of eleven and thirteen. They had been living on the streets until these Christians brought them into their program and started to show them something of the love of Christ. Quite suddenly, however, these girls stopped showing up and could not be found in their usual hangouts on the streets. After asking around, the missionaries heard that the girls had been abducted into a brothel. There they would be raped several times a day for the greed of others. Worse yet, the missionaries were informed that the brothel was being run by the local police.

As it turns out, their story provides us with just a glimpse of this "incredibly bad world." The vastness of the injustice that international Christian workers encounter is truly staggering. Each year, for example, more than a million children around the world are forced into prostitution—a million *new* children each year. It is nearly impossible to get our minds wrapped around the human magnitude of these numbers.

Lately I have been gaining a more concrete vision of the way this must appear to our all-knowing God. Not long ago I was able to look physically on a gathering of a *million* men on the mall in Washington, D.C., at the solemn assembly convened by the Promise Keepers ministry. In the midst of that seemingly endless crush of humanity, I felt a deep sadness come over me. I realized that over the coming year the same number of children would be packed into the world's darkest brothels.

Abusive child labor. Prostitution is just one of the abuses that confront vulnerable children of our world. In our survey, every third mission agency reported that they were also serving in communities that allowed abusive child labor. Perhaps the story of just one little girl will help us understand what Christians working throughout the world know.

World Vision India, a Christian relief and development agency, recently introduced me to a ten-year-old girl in a little village in the state of Tamil Naidu. Her name is Kanmani. From 8:00 in the morning until 6:00 at night, six days a week, she sits in the same little place on the floor and manufactures cigarettes. Her job is to close the ends with a little knife. She is required to complete 2,000 cigarettes a day. If she doesn't work fast enough, her overseer strikes her on the head. Her ten-hour work day is broken only by a single thirty-minute lunch period. At the end of a long week she gets her wages—about seventy-five cents. Worst of all, she has been working like this for more than *five* years.

Kanmani is a bonded laborer. That means she has to work like this to pay off a family debt. In a moment of economic crisis her family had to borrow about fifty dollars. To secure the loan, Kanmani's parents had to agree to send her to work for the moneylender. The agreement, however, requires that the debt be paid back in a lump sum, so even if Kanmani's family never spent any of her wages, it would take more than a year to pay back the debt. Of course, her family desperately needs Kanmani's seventy-five cents each week, so five years later Kanmani is no closer to paying off the debt than when she started. Without intervention she will spend her entire childhood this way.

We met several others in Kanmani's village: Pallavi, a nine-year-old girl, bonded for a twenty-five dollar loan to pay a medical bill when her father got sick; Jayanthi, a thirteen-year-old girl, bonded for the last eight years, working eleven hours a day for a fifty dollar debt;

Mubeena, an eight-year-old girl, working fourteen hours a day to pay off a thirty-five-dollar family debt; and Jabeena, a nine-year-old girl, working twelve hours a day to pay off a twenty-five-dollar debt incurred when her family of three brothers were sick with fever.

As inconceivable as it may seem, their story is repeated in India several *million* times over as destitute families are forced to sell their children into indefinite servitude by the lies and threats of those who traffic in child labor. Just as it says in the ancient Scriptures, so it is today, "the infant of the poor is seized for a debt" (Job 24:9). And all of this goes on despite the fact that such practices have been illegal under Indian law since the 1930s.

Evil at work the world over. Indeed, it is not difficult to "look out over the wide lands" just beyond each fair garden and see what an "incredibly bad world" it is. Consider this brief tour around the globe.

Slavery. In the Sudan a Canadian Christian television program recently bought and freed 319 women and children slaves in Southern Sudan. The television crew filmed the purchase of the slaves. They were sold for about $108 each.[1]

Murder and corruption. In April 1996 state police in northern Brazil killed nineteen landless peasants—ten were summarily executed, three shot at point-blank range and seven killed with knives or sickles. In the first eight months of 1996 forty-five landless peasants were killed by the private thugs of landowners in Brazil. According to the U.S. State Department, "Such killings usually go unpunished, because the landowners thought to be responsible for many of them reportedly control the police in isolated areas and intimidate local judges and lawyers with violence and threats of violence."[2]

Abusive police and forced prostitution. A Christian ministry leader recently told me about a hollow-eyed woman in Indonesia he had recently met. Looking at her, he guessed she was in her fifties. In fact, she is barely thirty years old. For the last several years her husband has been languishing in a filthy Indonesian jail. His survival depends on her visits and extra provisions, but in order to exercise her visitation rights, she must prostitute herself to six different prison guards. She is getting old very quickly.

Detention or disappearance without charge or trial. In 1996 in Kenya, "police continued to commit extrajudicial killings and to torture and beat detainees. . . . Through the spring and summer . . . government harassment and intimidation of opponents significantly increased."[3]

State-sponsored torture. In 1996 in Turkey, torture remained "widespread," with frequent police abuse during detention and interrogation. A "climate of impunity" is present as convictions of police or officials for killings or torture are rare.[4]

No doubt about it, as it was in the third century so it is at the beginning of the twenty-first: this is an "incredibly bad world."

But, honestly, what are we supposed to do with this information?

Don't despair, take heart! In a matter of seconds, we can go from knowing next to nothing about children in India to knowing that fifteen *million* of them are enslaved in short, brutal, dead-end lives of bonded servitude. Now what? In our hearts we feel like deer frozen by headlights. The very information that should move us is so overwhelming that it actually paralyzes. It is like a big meal that is supposed to provide fuel for our body but actually makes us feel like lying down and taking a nap. Instead of energizing us for action, the overwhelming injustice in our world actually makes us feel numb. We sense our hearts melting and our feet sinking into concrete.

This is when we need to listen to the voice of Jesus, the Jesus who encouraged the paralytic to "take heart!" (Matthew 9:22). When their spirits are crippled by the sheer weight of the world's injustice, Jesus tells his disciples, "Take heart! I have overcome the world" (John 16:33). He makes this declaration, however, not that we might sit cheerfully in our paralysis but that we might actually get up and walk. Even to the lame, Jesus begins with a straightforward question: "Do you wish to get well?" (John 5:6). Likewise, Jesus calls us to a moment of honest reflection. Do we really want to move to a new place? Do we really want to stand before a needy world free of all hindrances of the heart? Do we really want to see the world with the heart of Jesus and the courage of his Spirit?

Of course we do. But we often do not know how to go from awareness to action.

The Second Step: Preparing Our Mind for Action

As one who wept over his own faintness of heart, the apostle Peter urges us to begin by preparing our minds for action (Matthew 26:69-75; 1 Peter 1:13). Such preparation comes from a return to biblical truth. In particular we need to see what the Bible says about the world's true nature and its real needs.

The Bible declares that the world is fallen, sinful. Often I am ill-prepared for action in a dark world of injustice because I have gotten used to a little lie within my mind. I have gotten used to the idea that the fair garden that I have worked so hard to carve out for myself and my family is normal. I have gradually adjusted to the idea that "the world" into which Christ has sent his disciples is actually a reasonably pleasant backyard patio. Certainly it is no Garden of Eden—there are unruly shrubs, unpleasant neighbors, rainy days, tearful nights and even vandals. But in my garden the Fall is being managed. Gradually in my mind "the world" referred to in the Bible is defined more and more by the boundary hedges I share with my neighbors. Accordingly, I hone my Christian witness for engagement in this domesticated garden. I come to see the full armor of God as battle dress for fighting weeds, backyard pests and trespassers.

Having strayed in my mind so far from the truth of Scripture, I am caught totally off guard when the true nature of "the world" passes before my eyes. When confronted with the massive, violent oppression in our world, I feel that something has gone wrong and that things are out of control. I feel like I've made a wrong turn and I'm out of place. Even in moments when I am feeling most earnest about my faith and convinced of God's power and presence in my life and in the world, when I am forced to consider the millions of men, women and children who suffer the great brutalities of injustice in this world, I feel disoriented. I may have assembled something of a Christian world-view, but when the evening news shows the weak of the world being beaten up so badly on such a massive scale, I feel vaguely like I'm not where I'm supposed to be.

"Oh, but you are!" says Jesus. And this is the point. Preparing our mind for action means coming to grips with the true nature of the world into which Christ has cast us, his disciples. It means coming to grips with how the Fall is playing itself out around the world in the present day. When humanity rejected its Maker—the very God of love, mercy, justice, goodness and compassion—it set on the throne the human will to power. The outcome in the twentieth century could be described in various ways, but I would just call it an open-mouthed grave: an entire generation of European youth composting the World War I battlefields of Verdun and the Somme, Hitler's six million Jews, Stalin's twenty million Soviet citizens, Mao's tens of millions of political enemies and peasant famine victims, Pol Pot's two million Cambodians, the Interhamwe's million Tutsi Rwandans, and the millions of lives wasted away during apartheid's forty-year reign.

We can easily forget that the same spirit of darkness rules our present age. In the affluent West it manifests itself in a spiritual barrenness that made non-Western Christians like Mother Theresa and Aleksandr Solzhenitsyn gasp and grieve. For these Eastern Christians, Western brokenness and deathlike alienation from the sacred evokes a guttural reaction not unlike that experienced by Americans and Europeans at the sight of starving children. Outside the affluent West, however, in the Two-Thirds World where most of the children God created actually live, the Fall is being played out in ways more familiar to the biblical writers: it is manifest in a world of brutal injustice. As the apostle Paul wrote about the fallen world, quoting the prophet Isaiah and King David: "Their feet are swift to shed blood; ruin and misery mark their ways, and the way of peace they do not know. There is no fear of God before their eyes" (Romans 3:15-18).

Isaiah finished the same thought this way: "The way of peace they do not know; there is no justice in their paths. . . . No one who walks in them will know peace. So justice is far from us, and righteousness does not reach us. We look for light, but all is darkness" (Isaiah 59:7-9).

The Bible declares the world's need for salvation and justice. Biblical Christians understand that Christ has called us to be his witnesses to the uttermost part of a very dark world—a dark world of injustice. Preparing our minds for action in the world means coming to grips with the notion that the world into which we are sent as salt and light is a world that needs salt and light precisely because, among other things, it is full of the corruption and darkness of injustice. All those old Scriptures about "the world," which always seemed rather melodramatic when I heard them in my suburban church as a kid, turned out to be much more worthy of my attention than I ever knew.

Uncommon Courage for Common Christians: The Gift of God's Word

Much of my shock, disorientation and paralysis in the face of an unjust world simply comes from my failure to truly hide God's Word in my heart (Psalm 119:11). God intends that I face the world with courage, joy and a steady eye because of the truth of his Word. Through his Word God's people are given every advantage for living in the world, because despite deceitful appearances, the Bible tells the truth about the nature of the world and the nature of the God we serve.

These may not be our favorite passages of Scripture, and they may never get featured on our calendar of daily inspiration, but truth be told, the Bible is not coy about the kind of world into which Christ has sent his disciples.

> Men move boundary stones; they pasture flocks they have stolen. They drive away the orphan's donkey and take the widow's ox in pledge. They thrust the needy from the path and force all the poor of the land into hiding. . . . The fatherless child is snatched from the breast; the infant of the poor is seized for a debt. Lacking clothes, they go about naked; they carry the sheaves, but still go hungry. (Job 24:2-4, 9-10)

> The wicked draw the sword and bend the bow to bring down the poor and needy. (Psalm 37:14)

> It is you [the elders and princes] who have ruined my vineyard; the plunder from the poor is in your houses. (Isaiah 3:14)

> Women have been ravished in Zion, and virgins in the towns of Judah. Princes have been hung up by their hands; elders are shown no respect. Young men toil at the millstones; boys stagger under loads of wood. (Lamentations 5:11-13)

> The people of the land practice extortion and commit robbery; they oppress the poor and needy and mistreat the alien, denying them justice. (Ezekiel 22:29)

> They cast lots for my people and traded boys for prostitutes; they sold girls for wine that they might drink. (Joel 3:3)

> He [Ammon] ripped open the pregnant women of Gilead in order to extend his borders. (Amos 1:13)

The last people who should get caught off guard by injustice in the world should be Bible-believing Christians. For even as we celebrate the coming of Christ into the world, in Scripture we are powerfully reminded of the kind of world into which he has come. We seldom speak of it at Christmastime (although medieval Christians clearly did), but even the birth of Jesus was accompanied by one of the most brutal acts of injustice in history. As we may recall, King Herod felt threatened by the prospect of a new king of the Jews and "gave orders to kill all the boys in Bethlehem and its vicinity who were two years old and under" (Matthew 2:16). The early church numbered the victims in the thousands. In his Gospel the apostle Matthew hides nothing from our eyes. He treats us like grown-ups. He looks us straight in the eye and lets us know that ours is a world in which even a baby "away in a manger" is not safe from the brutal abuse of power.

The Bible could not be plainer: "If you see the poor oppressed in a district, and justice and rights denied, do not be surprised at such things" (Ecclesiastes 5:8). Thus the Word of God leads us in preparing our minds for action. Through his Word and through his Spirit, God speaks the word of truth that steadies our hearts for service in a difficult world. "Stand firm then, with the belt of truth buckled around your waist . . . and with your feet fitted with the readiness that comes from the gospel of peace" (Ephesians 6:14-15). We need not feel overwhelmed or out of place in such a dark world of injustice. This is precisely the world into which Jesus intended his followers to go. "You are the light of the world. . . . Let your light shine before men, that they may see your good deeds and praise your Father in heaven" (Matthew 5:14-16). Moreover, as we serve him in the world, Jesus assures us, "All authority in heaven and on earth has been given unto me. . . . And surely I am with you always, to the very end of the age" (Matthew 28:18-20).

Even so, as we take our first steps out of our familiar boat of safety and into the seas of a troubled and needy world, we can hear the words of our Master beckoning us, "Take courage! It is I. Don't be afraid" (Matthew 14:27).

Three

Champions
of Justice

Three Courageous Christians

IN *THE SCREWTAPE LETTERS,* AN INGENIOUS REFLECTION ON THE forces that drain the lifeblood from Christian faith, C. S. Lewis makes a startling statement. He writes that "Despair is a greater sin than any of the sins that provoke it."[1] And surely for Christians looking at our incredibly evil world of injustice and oppression, despair can always be found lurking at the door of our hearts, waiting to hobble us the moment we begin to take our first steps forward. After all, what can *we* do? How can *we* make a difference in a world of such massive and brutal injustice?

Strongholds of Injustice
Sister K., Brother E. and Sister J. know about the temptations of despair.

In Sister K.'s country there is a booming business in forced prostitution. The local police protect it and even hunt down girls who try to run away, often returning them to the stockades where they are held. Sister K. is personally aware of almost sixty brothels where she has found hundreds of young girls kept in subjection by "whip, fist, boot and bulldog"—some girls only thirteen and fourteen years old.

A state-appointed investigator assigned to look into the issue visited a single brothel and concluded that there was "no necessity for state interference in the matter." But Sister K. knows differently, and the brutal reality is beyond comprehension. She learned that one of the women held in prostitution was actually murdered by being soaked in oil and burned alive. The coroner's report of her death even named the perpetrator. It read: "Burned to death by W. H. Griffin." But the man was never charged with a crime. Local politicians prevent any legal action from being taken against the forced prostitution rings because they owe their position and influence to the wealthy business interests behind the brothels.

In the face of such injustice what can Sister K. do?

In Brother E.'s country abusive child labor is a plague on the land. Where he lives, about two million children between the ages of ten and fifteen years old work in textile mills, tobacco-processing plants, mines and other factories. Children work twelve hours a day, six days a week, sometimes on dangerous night shifts. Some must endure working eighty-two hours per week in a factory during peak weeks of the year. Many of the girls work in silk mills just as the boys work as "breakers" in the coal mines. Every day the breaker boys breathe in the heavy soot that covers them as they pick the debris out of the coal by hand. According to one person, the children of the breakers and the mills are "stooped and skinny, often missing thumbs and fingers and always giving the impression of being older than they were. Only when they were maimed so seriously that they can no longer work did such children attend school." As a prominent national lawyer commented, "You sell your boys to be slaves of the breakers and your girls to be slaves in the mills."

In the face of such oppression what can Brother E. do?

In Sister J.'s country summary execution by mobs is a way of life.

The majority ethnic group maintains its dominance over the minority ethnic group through the intimidation of extrajudicial murder. Every year fifty, sixty or a hundred people are burned alive or hanged after being accused of committing some offense against the majority ethnic group. These brutal events are gruesome public affairs, often performed in the presence of local officials on the basis of a simple denunciation by a member of the majority group. Without any opportunity to defend themselves, the accused are hustled off to a terrifying death. Local law-enforcement officials simply refuse to intervene and occasionally carry out the executions themselves.

In the face of such brutal human-rights violations what can Sister J. do?

Sister K., Brother E. and Sister J. are very real people. The circumstances described are documented beyond any dispute. They are, in fact, part of history. Kate, Edgar and Jessie are actually devout Christians of another era, and the country in which they encountered such staggering injustice is the United States of America. But today, although Americans have certainly not purged injustice from their society, these conditions simply no longer exist, in large part because of the courageous obedience of Christians to the call of God. In the face of brutal injustice and oppression that rivals anything anywhere on our globe today, courageous Christians simply refused to despair. Thankfully, America has never been the same.

Kate Bushnell: Abolishing Forced Prostitution

A hundred years ago Dr. Kate Bushnell served as a national evangelist for the Women's Christian Temperance Union (WCTU) in the United States. A devout evangelical Christian, Dr. Kate Bushnell was heartbroken by the plight of girls victimized by white slavery in America. Hard as it may be to imagine today, the dens of forced prostitution described earlier were rampant in the logging camps and mining communities of northern Wisconsin and Michigan in the 1880s. It was in Ashland, Wisconsin, that Dr. Bushnell encountered the murder of the woman who was burned alive with impunity.

While in some cases police responded to the pleas of women who were seeking to escape their bondage, other times they didn't listen and even returned runaways to their brothels. The existence of these dens and dance halls of rape was largely supported by the local community. The owners and patrons of such establishments exercised enough political power to prevent legal action against the brothels. Local doctors supported their existence because their frequent examination of the women provided a source of additional income. And local businessmen found that brothels provided a boost to the local economy.

Dr. Bushnell looked in vain for someone to properly investigate these conditions. Finding no one willing to take the risks, she did it herself. Facing tremendous personal danger, she infiltrated scores of brothels and interviewed hundreds of women held in bondage. "She would search for reliable witnesses having personal knowledge of an involvement in the case under investigation. She insisted on talking to inmates, viewing the situation herself. One side of the story, from one witness, was not enough. . . . Having penetrated the brothel by one excuse or another, she was able by various pretexts to obtain proof of the conditions that existed there."[2]

Dr. Bushnell reported her findings at a Chicago convention of the WCTU. The state of Wisconsin vehemently denied her findings, and the state inspector even attempted to discredit her by accusing Dr. Bushnell herself of "unchastity." When she appeared before the Wisconsin state legislature, she had to be escorted by police because of threats of violence against her. Standing before the hostile assembly, she initially felt overwhelmed as the only woman in the room. But

being a woman of prayer, she lifted her heart to God, "whereupon the door opened quietly, and about fifty ladies of the highest social position at the State Capitol filed in, and stood all about me. There were no seats for them; they stood all the time I talked—and I had plenty of courage as I realized how good God was to send them."[3]

Despite the attacks on Dr. Bushnell and her study, "the whole country was agitated on the white slave question by the disclosures" she had made.[4] Her findings were substantiated by subsequent studies conducted by both public officials and private researchers. The result of her work was the passage of a bill in the Wisconsin legislature that finally dealt with the scourge of forced prostitution in a serious way. The bill was appropriately labeled "the Kate Bushnell Bill." Later Dr. Bushnell took her Christian witness to India and China, where she and other Christians challenged the complicity of British colonial officials in the rampant trafficking of women and girls in forced prostitution.

Edgar Murphy: Transforming the Destiny of Child Laborers

Today we look with horror and despair at reports of the millions of young children who toil under abusive labor conditions around the world. And yet at the turn of the century similar conditions were not uncommon in North America. Edgar Gardner Murphy, a minister of the gospel from Alabama, was certainly familiar with them. The Reverend Murphy was particularly burdened by the oppression suffered by the tens of thousands of children under age fourteen who toiled in the textile mills of his native American South. I found myself thinking of my sister's own six-year-old daughter as I encountered the comments of an observer from 1902 who described the fate of just one of these children.

> Mattie . . . is six years old. She is a spinner. Inside a cotton mill for 12 hours a day she stands in a 4-foot passage-way between the spinning frames where the cotton is spun from coarser into fine threads. . . . From daylight to dark she is in the midst of the

ceaseless throb and racket of machinery. When I first met her it was Christmas Eve. The eve of the children's festival when the whole of Christendom celebrates the birth of the Child whose coming was to bring freedom to children. She was crying, and when I asked the reason, she said between her sobs, that she wanted a doll that would open and shut its eyes. "When would you play with it?" I asked the little toiler, whose weary eyelids were ready to close over her tired eyes directly after the long day's work was over. "I should have time aplenty on Sunday," replied the little slave whose daily wage of ten cents helped to swell the family income.[5]

As a disciple of Jesus Christ, Rev. Murphy chose not to surrender to despair in the face of such a tragedy. In 1901 in response to his expanding knowledge of the atrocities of child labor in the mills, Murphy founded the Alabama Child Labor Committee. Rev. Murphy began to write to inform the public of the horrors he witnessed. He authored nine pamphlets on the subject and distributed twenty-eight thousand copies throughout the United States, often at his own personal expense. His writing effort has been called "the first body of printed material of any considerable extent or value" in favor of legislation restricting child labor in the American South.[6]

Rev. Murphy believed that children belonged in "God's outdoors, in the home, or in the schoolroom."[7] On one occasion Rev. Murphy examined a seven-year-old's hand that had had three fingers torn from it during dangerous mill work. When the mill owner explained that the child had been careless, Rev. Murphy replied, "Hasn't a child seven years of age got a right to be careless?"

In 1904 Murphy joined with other advocates of reform to found the National Child Labor Committee (NCLC). The NCLC came to be regarded as the most effective voice in bringing about the abolition of child labor in America, and Rev. Murphy is referred to by contemporaries and historians alike as its father and founder. Perhaps Murphy's greatest personal victory came, however, when his home state of Alabama finally issued legislative restrictions on child labor in 1907. Even more substantial, though probably unrecognized by Murphy himself, was the fact that he had "pricked the conscience of the country alive to the existence of child labor as a shame and a curse to America."[8] One man's faithful devotion to his Master's call to care for "the least of these" helped transform the destiny of millions of American children.

Enough Is Enough: Church Women and Lynching

In recent years summary executions by vigilante groups and "disappearances" by secret death squads have been among the uglier human-rights violations that have struck terror in the hearts of millions of people living in communities of social and political conflict around the world. Such state-sanctioned horror may seem distant, but there was a time not long ago, a time within the memory of many living Americans, when millions of their compatriots lived under such a threat.

In the first two decades of this century, thousands of African-American citizens were publicly lynched—including almost a hundred women. In four years, from 1918 to 1921, twenty-eight African-Americans were burned at the stake by mob action.[9] As late as the 1940s lynching was still a common method of social control and intimidation in the Southern states. But again it was the courageous faith of devout Christian women who helped bring this scourge to an end.

In the segregated South the practice of lynching was largely defended as a means to protect the honor of white women. It was often perpetrated against African-American men who were accused of raping a white woman or of simply addressing a white woman in a socially inappropriate fashion. Jessie Daniel Ames, a Southern white woman, believed that the most effective voice against lynching could come from those it was intended to benefit. In 1930 with only twelve compatriots, she created the Association of Southern Women for the Prevention of Lynching (ASWPL). These twelve women simply "went home and began to work and to talk and to retell the facts as they learned them."[10]

Ames and the other charter members were all officers in various Protestant denominations. Apart from the brutal injustice of the practice, they were deeply concerned that the lynching of African-Americans by white "Christians" tended to "discredit Christianity, and impede the work of missionaries among non-white peoples." As Ames later stated, "That was one of the strongest appeals we could make."[11]

Although Ames was its only salaried worker, the ASWPL had councils in all eleven former Confederate states and more than forty thousand active members. The key to her success seemed to be her reliance on volunteers and a preexisting network of religious and secular women's organizations, which provided cohesiveness for the ASWPL. By the early 1940s, 109 women's associations, representing 4 million women, supported the ASWPL's work. Not only did the women's organizations of the southern Protestant churches endorse ASWPL, but they also included antilynching literature in their respective educational materials.

Through literature, speeches and word of mouth within its vast network, ASWPL undermined the chivalric notions that fueled lynching and revealed the truth of the barbaric practice. They circulated petitions to show elected officials that there was widespread support for antilynching laws. They persuaded law-enforcement officials to sign a pledge expressing opposition to lynching. By 1941, 1,355 police officers had signed the pledge. Also in that year police officers in forty documented cases had successfully opposed lynch mobs. Furthermore, ASWPL exposed by name officers who failed to uphold the law. In some instances ASWPL women physically confronted the mobs. ASWPL members were credited with "preventing the lynching of scores of blacks, because of their timely phone calls to a sheriff or visits to a local jail."[12]

While Southern senators blocked federal antilynching legislation and thwarted any nationwide remedy, the ASWPL was able to fundamentally change the cultural mores and beliefs that undergirded the practice. And the impact was dramatic. As the distinguished Yale historian Dr. C. Vann Woodward has observed, "Efforts of civil rights groups to secure passage of federal anti-lynching laws failed repeatedly, but effective work by white and Negro groups, *many of them Southern church organizations,* virtually eliminated lynching for a time. The NAACP conceded the 'virtual disappearance of this form of oppression' in the early 1950s."[13] Of course the women of the ASWPL were not perfect and manifested many of the narrow attitudes common to many Southern white women of the day. Nevertheless, as one historian has commented on the era, "From its inception, the anti-lynching campaign was rooted firmly in a tradition of evangelical reform."[14]

Ordinary People, Extraordinary Faith

To me these stories are part of the great encouragement of a Christian heritage. Sometimes when I am utterly overwhelmed by the injustice in our world, recalling or reading about the faithful heroes of the past allows me to find my courage. When I raise my eyes, even for a moment, to the history of God's courage expressed in his people, I find hope and steadiness of heart.

Without the encouragement of stories like these, I can easily get buried in the intimidations of today. I can easily lose all perspective and hope. It makes me think of days as a small boy playing at the ocean and experiencing the terrific intimidation and disorientation of the waves as I waded farther and farther from the beach and other people. I vividly remember one occasion when, having been lulled to inattention by the temporary calm, a swelling wave blind-sided me without warning. It picked me up and rolled me over and over underwater. With something close to terror, I kicked and flailed my arms trying to swim to safety. Then just as wild panic began to grip my heart, my head was shoved above the surface just long enough to steal a glance down the shore line. There, very near me, were my two brothers, standing sturdily—in the same three feet of water in which I was flailing. Letting my feet float down, I quickly found the hard, sandy bottom and stood up—embarrassed a bit but greatly relieved.

Alone in the waves, I had lost perspective. Things were not as they appeared. The water felt infinitely deeper than it was. I had no idea of the sturdy ground that was actually well within reach. I felt helpless, lost and overwhelmed. And as long as I felt that way, I possessed neither the power nor the presence of mind to stand amid the waves.

Likewise, when I see the great forces of injustice that crash upon our world, I find myself going from moments of easy obliviousness to moments of total disorientation and despair. But it is in these moments that I need to look down the shoreline of history and see my brothers and sisters of the faith—Dr. Bushnell, Rev. Murphy, the Christian women of the ASWPL and so many others—standing amid the crashing waves. The injustice and oppression in the world is powerful, relentless and pervasive, but as these three faithful witnesses attest, we are neither without a foothold to withstand its blows nor powerless to rescue those pulled under by its force.

There is a testimony of great hope in seeing how God has used ordinary people—from all nations—extraordinary in their Christian faith, to bring rescue to those who were hurting.

What Can We Learn from Faithful Christians?

These champions of justice teach us a couple of truths which at times we may question: bringing about justice can be within our reach, and it is also an integral part of our faith.

First, we learn that *we can change things*. Our despair, cynicism and laziness may insist to us that nothing ever really changes and that we can never really make a difference. But on high we see a great cloud of witnesses stand to their feet with a different testimony. Rank upon rank of vulnerable and voiceless girls tell us that for them Dr. Bushnell's faithfulness to God made a difference. Legions of children, each with a name, stand to bless Rev. Murphy for his obedience to Christ. Likewise, in honor of the faithful Christians who took a stand, countless African-American families can testify to the difference it makes to live in an American South without lynching. Still more give thanks to God for Dr. Martin Luther King Jr. for the opportunity to live in a South without apartheid. Like the blind man healed by Jesus, these witnesses show little interest in quibbling over historical or theological complexities. They only offer simple stories about the difference faith can make: "One thing I do know. I was blind but now I see" (John 9:25).

We are not caught up in a Pollyanna-like dream of bringing heaven to earth and abolishing injustice. On the contrary, we know that an ocean of oppression will pound humanity until he whom "even the wind and waves obey" shall command the storm to cease (Matthew 8:27). Moreover, we know that there are waves of injustice in this world against which even the most faithful will not be saved. But still we do not despair. As Dr. Martin Luther King Jr. said at his commencement address at Springfield College, "The moral arc of the universe is long, but it bends toward justice."[15] Calling us to "action in hope," the great missiologist David Bosch declares that "like its Lord, the church-in-mission must take sides, *for* life and against death, for justice and against oppression."[16]

> Precisely the vision of God's triumph makes it impossible to look for sanctuary in quietism, neutrality, or withdrawal from the field of action. We may never overrate our own capabilities; and yet, we may have confidence about the direction into which history moves, for we are not, like Sartre, peering into the abyss of nothingness, nauseated by the emptiness of our freedom, leaping into a future which only confirms the meaninglessness of the present moment.[17]

In the words of the apostle Paul, "Let us not become weary in doing good, for at the proper time we will reap a harvest if we do not give up" (Galatians 6:9). This is not a vague affirmation about the happy ending of history, the evolving goodness of man, the triumph of the scientific mind or the promise of a civilized world. It is a bedrock conviction about the nature of God and what it means to serve him in faithfulness. As he gives us eyes to see those in need, we will simply respond in love. As Bosch declared, "We hope because of what we have already experienced. Christian hope is both possession and yearning, repose and activity, arrival and being on the way. Since God's victory is certain, believers can work both patiently and enthusiastically, blending careful planning with urgent obedience, motivated by the patient impatience of the Christian hope."[18]

Second, we learn from Dr. Bushnell, Rev. Murphy and the Christian ladies of the ASWPL that *the biblical mandate to seek justice and rescue the oppressed is an integral and magnificent theme of the Christian heritage* (Isaiah 1:17). They may be unfamiliar to us now, but many of the greatest heroes of biblical Christianity in history were fully engaged in the work of seeking justice.

It would never have occurred to the great evangelicals of the nineteenth-century who battled so bravely to abolish slavery—William Wilberforce, Charles Finney, William Lloyd Garrison, Edward Beecher, Elijah Lovejoy, Theodore Dwight Weld—that Jesus could be honored by a life of Christian devotion that did not include a response of Christian love to those who are oppressed. For some it was precisely their conversion to Christ that moved them to take up the slavery cause. For John Gregg Fee, the evangelical founder of Berea College in Kentucky, it was while on his knees in anguished prayer that he confronted the costs of discipleship. "I saw that to embrace the principle of abolition and wear the name was to cut myself off from relatives and former friends." But he prayed, "Lord, if needs be, make me an Abolitionist." Later he said that he rose from prayer that day "with the consciousness that I had died to the world and accepted Christ in all the fullness of his character as I then understood him."[19]

In fact, historians have long recognized that the great achievements in humanitarian reform and social justice in the West during the nineteenth century—the abolition of slavery, prison reform, the establishment of hospitals and schools for the poor, women's rights, opposition to forced prostitution, the fight against child labor—were largely built on the faithful zeal of evangelical Christians. As American historian Sydney Ahlstrom of Yale University explained about that great humanitarian movement, "If the collective conscience of evangelical America is left out, the movement as a whole is incomprehensible." It was built, he said, on "the Puritan's basic confidence that the world could be constrained and re-formed in accordance with God's revealed will," and fueled by the revivalists' "demand for holiness, [and their] calling for socially relevant Christian commitment as the proper sequel to conversion."[20]

Recovering Our Ministry of Justice

In a detour away from biblical faith many Christians in the twentieth century neglected this heritage of service to a hurting world. As Bosch observed,

> It was a stupendous victory of the evil one to have made us believe that structures and conditions in this world will not or need not really change, to have considered political and societal powers and other vested interests inviolable, to have acquiesced in conditions of injustice and oppression, to have tempered our expectation to the point of compromise, to have given up the hope for a wholesale transformation of the status quo, to have been blind to our own responsibility for and involvement in a world en route to its fulfillment.[21]

But Christ has not neglected us, and now he calls us to recover the ministry of justice that once was ours. As the great evangelical theologian Carl F. H. Henry has said of evangelicals of the eighteenth and nineteenth centuries, their

> evangelical movement was spiritually and morally vital because it strove for justice and also invited humanity to regeneration, forgiveness, and power for righteousness. If the church preaches only divine forgiveness and does not affirm justice, she implies that God treats immorality and sin lightly. If the church proclaims only justice, we shall all die in unforgiven sin and without the spirit's empowerment for righteousness. We should be equally troubled that we lag in championing justice and in fulfilling our evangelistic mandate.[22]

As we peer down the halls of Christian history, we give thanks for those great champions of justice and evangelism who give us hope. For God intends that we remember his ancient work in equipping his people "to act justly and to love mercy and to walk humbly" (Micah 6:8). As the psalmist urges us, "Look to the LORD and his strength; seek his face always. Remember the wonders he has done, his miracles, and the judgments he pronounced" (Psalm 105:4-5).

And even as we remember, we lift our eyes to the horizon and ask, What great work of justice might God perform through us, in our time, to the glory of Christ? How might God renew through us the witness for biblical justice in the world? What child in bonded labor in India, what girl held in prostitution in Manila, what innocent man rotting in a Kenyan jail might yet stand and testify that the hand of a faithful God touched them and loved them through the obedience of Christians who refused to despair?

Part 2

Hope amid Despair

*God's Four Affirmations
About Injustice*

Four

Hope in the God of Justice

THE BATTLE FOR JUSTICE IN THE WORLD IS NOT FOUGHT where we think it is. The struggle against injustice is not fought on the battlefield of power or truth or even righteousness. There are pitched battles waged on these ramparts, but the war is ultimately won or lost on a more forward front. In the end the battle against oppression stands or falls on the battlefield of hope.

No one knows this better than the oppressors. They know that they never have enough power, lies or loyalty to withstand the onslaught of even a fraction of the power, truth and courage that humanity could at any minute amass against them. Therefore they rely on, utterly depend on, the inaction of despair. They know full well that their preeminence depends on most people in their community, their nation and their world doing nothing. This is the essence of Edmund Burke's conviction about human history: "All that is necessary for the triumph of evil is for good men to do nothing."

The oppressor knows that the primary reason we do nothing is because we have lost any hope of making a difference. It is not that we lack power, compassion, courage or knowledge. Rather, we lack a sense of hope that allows us to take what we have into the fray. By sheer inertia, therefore, we lend our own weight to the downward cycle of despair. Our lack of hope keeps us from the front lines of engagement. And our absence only makes the oppressor look stronger, compounding our own despair and that of those who might otherwise be prepared to fight.

But as faithful Christians through the ages have demonstrated, we don't have to be this way. We have access to a hope that changes everything. Great people of the faith—William Wilberforce and Dr. Martin Luther King Jr.—and lesser-known giants like Dr. Bushnell and Rev. Murphy changed their communities, their nation and their world because they found the hope to seek justice.

My Hope Is in God

Where did they find such hope? Where can we find such hope today? Where can we find a hope solid enough for action when we are surrounded by injustice? I don't know where others find their hope, but I have found mine where Wilberforce, King, Bushnell, Murphy and the ancient psalmist found theirs: I have put my hope in the word of God (Psalm 119:147).

As one who has with his own hands sorted through the remains of thousands of slaughtered Tutsi corpses, as one who has heard with his own ears the screams of boys being beaten like dogs by South African police, as one who has looked with his own eyes into the dull, blank stares of Asian girls abused in subhuman ways, I hope in the Word of God. For in the Scriptures and in the life of Jesus Christ, I have come to know God—my Maker, the Creator of heaven and earth, the sovereign Lord of the nations. It is through his Word that God reveals his character, and it is God's character, and God's character alone, that gives me hope to seek justice amid the brutality I witness.

This hope is not cheap, nor is it easy. In a genuinely fallen world Jesus neither offers us cheap grace nor cheap hope. But it is a hope honest enough to contend with the ugly oppression of our world, and it is a hope that has power to prevail against the worst that hell can bring to earth.

Make no mistake: nothing challenges one's faith and hope in God like the rank evil of naked injustice. And nothing short of the authoritative, divine Word of God will withstand its withering scorn. Every Christian worldview, Western ideology and personal conviction ultimately will be obliterated by the painful questions posed by harsh oppression—unless bolted soundly and solely to the Word of God. As Katherine Bushnell, the courageous champion against the brutalities of forced prostitution, once wrote: "We are mistaken if we think that we can get along with slovenly and incomplete knowledge of the Bible. No amount of spiritual experience, or even the Spirit's help and instruction, will take the place of the *study* God requires us to put upon His Word."[1]

Do we know the Word of God like that? What do we know about the nature of the God who rules the earth and holds our eternal destiny? What do we know about how he feels about injustice, about the downtrodden and about us Christians? Scripture offers answers for these and other questions, but they are rarely easy in their deepest applications, nor are they without mystery or even sorrow this side of heaven. But God has given us the words of hope. This is no small gift; for it is hope, more than anything else, that we need.

Four Truths About God's Character

Amid a world of injustice, oppression and abuse, we can know some simple truths about God if we study his Word. No matter what the circumstances, we can depend on what he has revealed about himself. In regard to injustice our heavenly Father bids us to trust in four solid truths about his character.

☐ God loves justice and, conversely, hates injustice.

☐ God has compassion for those who suffer injustice—everywhere around the world, without distinction or favor.

☐ God judges and condemns those who perpetrate injustice.

☐ God seeks active rescue for the victims of injustice.

These four truths are deceptively easy to state, but in a world like ours they often seem hard to believe and even harder to live by. Jesus, however, desperately wanted us to know that the truth will make us free and equip us to stand firm amid evil.

In this chapter we will see what the Scriptures say about the first of these truths—that God is a God of justice. Chapters five, six and seven show how the remaining three truths offer us hope and empower us to act against injustice.

Justice: The Right Exercise of Power

The centerpiece of our hope is the revelation from the Almighty that he is a God of justice. As the prophet Isaiah declared, "The LORD is a God of justice. Blessed are all who wait for him!" (Isaiah 30:19). Justice is fundamental to the holiness of God. "For I, the LORD, love justice," declares our Maker (Isaiah 61:8).

But what does this mean? What does God mean when he says he is a God of justice? What is "justice" anyway?

Before we seek some useful answers to these questions, one caution might be helpful. It would be ironic if, in our pursuit of hope, we immediately lost our way in the quagmire of semantics. In my over-educated experience few questions have generated more heat and less light than the inquiry into the "true" meaning of *justice.* If by our inquiry into the meaning of *justice* we are looking for the definition of a magic word, we will be most disappointed.

I remember as a boy of nine or ten being detained for some minor indiscretion during recess in my school library. There I discovered the wonderfully obese *Oxford English Dictionary.* I had looked up all the slang words I could think of when I began to discover where the writers seemed to be cheating. I found words like *life,* which they said meant "being," but when I looked up *being,* they just said it meant "life." I thought, *How unhelpful.*

What I had discovered, of course, is that although a dictionary is supposed to tell us the meaning of words, every word is defined only by other words. *Life* is a word, but a dictionary can tell us next to nothing about the "meaning of life." Likewise, a meaningful understanding of "justice" or of a "just God" does not emerge from a neat, all-purpose definition of the word *justice.*

Some of us grow so frustrated by the fact that something as important and wonderful as justice cannot be reduced to a handy word formula that we begin to give up on justice—believing that something so vague cannot be so important or wonderful after all, even concluding that it probably doesn't actually exist. Similarly, some people find the meaning of life so elusive that they also give up on its pursuit. But we call this suicide. We should not be likewise tempted into despair about the pursuit of justice because of the limits of our vocabulary.

Having said that, what does it mean to say that ours is a God of justice? Is there anything that we can usefully understand about justice in the Bible? I believe there is. Fundamentally, justice has to do with the exercise of power. To say that God is a God of justice is to say that he is a God who cares about the right exercise of power or authority. God is the ultimate power and authority in the universe, so justice occurs when power and authority is exercised in conformity with his standards. In fact, in the Old Testament the Hebrew words for justice and righteousness are almost interchangeable, both indicating a conformity to God's standards of holiness or moral excellence. Ultimately, the sovereign God of the universe will establish justice over all peoples and spirits because at that time all power and authority in the cosmos will be exercised in accordance with his standards of moral purity.

So justice occurs on earth when power and authority between people is exercised in conformity with God's standards of moral excellence. There is always a distribution of power among people in every human society—some have more, some have less. All kinds of power is distributed: political, economic, social, moral, religious, cultural, familial, coercive, intellectual and so on. To say that God is a God of justice is one way of saying that he is concerned about whether those who have power or authority over others are exercising it in accordance with his standards. When power is exercised in a way that violates those standards we call it *injustice.*

Injustice: The Abuse of Power
When does the use of power violate God's standards of moral excellence? What is injustice? Here again, no one-size-fits-all definition is available to us, but the biblical text does seem to provide a rather consistent, thematic definition. *Injustice occurs when power is misused to take from others what God has given them, namely, their life, dignity, liberty or the fruits of their love and labor.*

Typically the Bible defines its core concepts not so much with elaborate definitions but with stories: love (the Good Samaritan), faith (Abraham's offering of Isaac), grace (the prodigal son). One of the best examples of the Bible's simple definition of injustice comes from the only teaching parable of the Old Testament—the prophet Nathan's story of the rich man who uses his power to steal the poor man's only lamb. Nathan told this story to describe to David the grave injustice he had committed in using his kingly power to take Uriah's wife and then to arrange Uriah's death.

Fundamentally, injustice is about the abuse of power. As it says in Ecclesiastes, "Again I looked and saw all the oppression that was taking place under the sun: I saw the tears of the oppressed—and they have no comforter; power was on the side of their oppressors" (Ecclesiastes 4:1). Injustice is the strong using force and deceit to take from the weak.

When I worked for the police-misconduct task force of the U.S. Department of Justice, my job was to confront injustice committed by police officers—officers who abused their power to take what was not theirs from vulnerable citizens. One case dealt with a young teenage girl who had run away from her abusive home in the country to seek refuge on the streets of a big city in the South. One evening the young girl had gotten herself in a difficult situation on the street, and a police car pulled up to lend her a hand. She was nervous about getting in trouble for being a runaway, but being homeless she accepted the offer of the two policemen to put her up in a motel for the night. With a mixture of fear and hope that she might find safety with these two officers, she slid her small frame into the back of the squad car. When they arrived at the motel, one of the officers retrieved a room key, walked her to the door and escorted her in. But instead of leaving, the officer forced her onto the bed and raped her. After a while the other officer entered the room, and for a moment the girl thought that she had found a rescue. Instead, she found another rapist. When the two policemen finished, they put her back in the car and dumped her on the street.

This is injustice: the strong preying on the weak. These officers used the authority of their position to obtain her young trust. Then they used the power of their coercive strength to rob her of what God had given her—her dignity as a child made in the image of God, the inviolability of her body as a temple of the Holy Spirit and her freedom to be known only by the soul mate chosen by her heart.

Such injustice is the plague of our earth. It occurs every day around the world. Immoral soldiers take people's dignity, freedom, health and well-being through beatings, torture and incarceration. Corrupt authorities and moneylenders rob children of their childhood, health, innocence and joy through abusive servitude. Wealthy landowners rob widows of their land, livelihood and dignity. Brutal bigots in positions of power take away the loved ones, the livelihood and even the very lives of those who are of a different race, religion, gender or culture. Even today, as I write, I read in the newspaper that more than sixty men, women and children of low-caste peasant families in India were

murdered in their sleep by the private army of local high-caste landowners to enforce acknowledgment of their supremacy.[2]

The oppressors who commit these acts do not believe in God or in
his need for justice. They think that no one cares and no one will
interfere with their plans.

In arrogance the wicked persecute the poor. . . .

For the wicked boast of the desires of their heart,
    those greedy for gain curse and renounce the LORD.
In the pride their countenance the wicked say, "God will not seek
    it out." . . .

Their eyes stealthily watch for the helpless;
    they lurk in secret like a lion in his covert;
they lurk that they may seize the poor;
    they seize the poor and drag them off in their net.

They stoop, they crouch,
    and the helpless fall by their might.
They think in their heart, "God has forgotten,
    he has hidden his face, he will never see it."
        (Psalm 10:2-4, 8-11 NRSV)

How Does God Regard Such Suffering?

The Word of God tells us God has not forgotten injustice or the
suffering of the victims. "Why," asks the psalmist, "does the wicked
man revile God? Why does he say to himself, 'He won't call me to
account'? But you, O God, do see trouble and grief; you consider it to
take it in hand. The victim commits himself to you; you are the helper
of the fatherless" (Psalm 10:13-14). The oppressors could not be
further from the truth: God does care.

All of the biblical teaching about the God of justice can be summed
up in a simple affirmation: God hates injustice and wants it to stop.

This truth is fundamental to the nature of our God, and the Bible makes clear that those who do not understand this aspect of God's holiness simply do not know God. "For I, the LORD love justice; I hate robbery and iniquity" (Isaiah 61:8). God's interest in the abuse of power is not mild. Nor is he at all resigned to injustice in a fallen world. The use of power by the strong to abuse the weak strikes at the very core of his holy heart.

While we may have grown numb or oblivious to much of the brutal abuse of our world, God maintains a fresh, holy hatred of injustice. "God is a righteous judge, a God who expresses his wrath every day" (Psalm 7:11). And "the LORD examines the righteous, but the wicked and those who love violence his soul hates. On the wicked he will rain fiery coals and burning sulfur; a scorching wind will be their lot. For the LORD is righteous, he loves justice" (Psalm 11:5-7).

If we want to know God, to really understand him, we must come to understand his passion for justice and his gut-level indignation at the abuse of power. "This is what the LORD says: 'Let not the wise man boast of his wisdom or the strong man boast of his strength or the rich man boast of his riches, but let him who boasts boast about this: that he understands and knows me, that I am the LORD, who exercises kindness, *justice* and righteousness on earth, for in these I delight' " (Jeremiah 9:23-24).

Just how well do we know our God? Our passion for justice and the defense of the weak will reflect it. " 'Did not your father . . . do justice and righteousness? Then it was well with him. He pled the cause of the afflicted and needy; then it was well. Is not that what it means to know me?' declares the LORD" (Jeremiah 22:15-16 NASB). Jesus certainly understood the character of his heavenly Father. Jesus saved his harshest words for the Pharisees who claimed great knowledge of God but neglected "the more important matters" of God's law: "justice, mercy and faithfulness" (Matthew 23:23). In the words of Solomon, "The evil do not understand

justice, but those who seek the LORD understand it completely"
(Proverbs 28:5).

I have never heard the point made more clearly than when I heard
Joseph Stowell, president of Moody Bible Institute, speak to the
leaders of evangelical mission agencies. He began by describing how
terrible it would be to grow up with a father who never told us what
pleased him and what he expected of us. As much as we might love
him, we could never have the joy of making him happy if he never
told us what he liked and disliked, and therefore what he would like
from us. Stowell went on to say how wonderful it was that our
heavenly Father wasn't like that and what a blessing it is that he tells
us precisely what makes him happy and what he expects from us.
Stowell then directed our attention to the prophet Micah who set forth
these requirements with crystal clarity: "He has told you, O mortal,
what is good; and what does the LORD require of you but to do justice,
and to love kindness, and to walk humbly with your God?" (Micah
6:8 NRSV). Here we have set forth the heart of God, and the short
list begins with justice.

Claiming the Hope: Desiring and Doing Justice

Our God loves justice. This is the great hope that allows Christians to
be a mighty force for justice in a tired, despairing world. For many of
us, however, this hope in the character of a just God often lies forgotten
and fallow in the neglected corners of our hearts. Unwittingly we
become the hoarders of hidden hope.

We are like the widow in California I heard about who after her
husband's death allowed her family to slide into financial ruin simply
because she refused to believe what her lawyers told her about the
fortune her husband had secreted away in a local bank. Over time the
unemployed widow couldn't pay her bills, got evicted from her home
and wandered about the county with her children—homeless, ill-fed
and ill-clothed. They were destitute, all because she simply refused to

believe in her inheritance. And there it sat, hundreds of thousands of dollars. The money was truly hers, but it could do her no good until she claimed it.

Likewise, our great inheritance of hope from a God of justice does us and the world no good unless we claim it. When we can truly believe the testimony of the Scriptures and of Jesus Christ that our heavenly Father is a God of justice, we are equipped to be light in a dark world. The hope is truly ours; we just have to claim it. We have a great witness for a weary world, if we are simply willing to believe.

> Blessed is he whose help is the God of Jacob,
>   whose hope is in the LORD his God,
> the Maker of heaven and earth,
>   the sea, and everything in them—
>   the LORD, who remains faithful forever.
> He upholds the cause of the oppressed
>   and gives food to the hungry.
> The LORD sets prisoners free,
>   The LORD gives sight to the blind,
> the LORD lifts up those who are bowed down,
>   the LORD loves the righteous.
> The LORD watches over the alien
>   and sustains the fatherless and the widow,
>   but he frustrates the ways of the wicked.
> The LORD reigns forever,
>   your God, O Zion, for all generations.
> Praise the LORD. (Psalm 146:5-10)

Five

Hope in the God of Compassion

THE SECOND FUNDAMENTAL TRUTH THAT GOD WANTS US TO count on in a world of injustice is that God has compassion for those who suffer injustice. Again this truth is infinitely easier to state than it is to believe—especially during the long stretches of silence when we picture the cries of the oppressed arcing out from the earth only to be lost in a dark, endless void that neither hears nor speaks.

We who know God, however, trust that he hears and cares, for he is a God of compassion. The cries of those who suffer injustice move him. We have hope because we know we serve such a God. "Our God is full of compassion," says the psalmist (Psalm 116:5). He is "the Father of compassion," says the apostle Paul (2 Corinthians 1:3).

The word *compassion* comes from two Latin words: *passio*, meaning "to suffer," and *cum*, meaning "with." To say that God has compassion for the victims of injustice is to say that he actually "suffers with" them.[1] At the root of God's compassion is the fact that he sees, witnesses, directly observes the suffering of the abused.

God's Presence amid the Suffering

When it comes to the brutality of injustice in our fallen world, there is no place for an all-knowing God to hide—a God who "has compassion on all he has made" (Psalm 145:9). When the Israelites were oppressed in Egypt, God told Moses, "I have indeed seen the misery of my people in Egypt. I have heard them crying out because of their slave drivers, and I am concerned about their suffering" (Exodus 3:7). Today when the taskmaster beats the seven-year-old bonded child laborer in India for not rolling his quota of cigarettes, God sees and hears. When the two police officers rape the runaway girl, he witnesses it. When mobs mercilessly hack to death thousands of Tutsi women and children, he suffers with them.

Over and over in the Scriptures God lets us know that he sees and hears the suffering of the oppressed. When the strong abuse their power to take from those who are weaker, the sovereign God of the universe is watching, and suffering.

> If you take your neighbor's cloak as a pledge, return it to him by sunset, because his cloak is the only covering he has for his body. What else will he sleep in? When he cries out to me, I will hear, for I am compassionate. (Exodus 22:26-27)

> The LORD is a refuge for the oppressed. . . . He does not ignore the cry of the afflicted. (Psalm 9:9, 12)

> "Because of the oppression of the weak and the groaning of the needy, I will now arise," says the LORD. "I will protect them from those who malign them." (Psalm 12:5)

> To deprive a man of justice—would not the Lord see such things? (Lamentations 3:36).

Look! The wages you failed to pay the workmen who mowed
your fields are crying out against you. The cries of the harvesters
have reached the ears of the Lord Almighty. (James 5:4)

Why God Passionately Hates Injustice

Coming to understand God's compassion for the oppressed, and the
way he suffers with them, has completely transformed my understanding of God. His real presence amid the horrendous injustice of
our earth has finally allowed me to understand why God *hates* injustice
so much. I have had to imagine what it would be like if I, like my God,
had to watch, hear and witness every brutal act of injustice on the earth,
every day.

In Rwanda, where I had to bear the burden of digging through the
twisted, reeking remains of horrific mass graves, I tried to imagine,
for just a minute, what it must have been like for God to be present at
each of the massacre sites as thousands of Tutsi women and children
were murdered. Frankly, the idea was impossible to bear. But the
thought lead me to imagine what it must be like for God to be present,
this year, at the rape of all the world's child prostitutes, at the beatings
of all the world's prisoners of conscience, at the moment the last breath
of hope expires from the breast of each of the millions of small
children languishing in bonded servitude. As I would approach my
God in prayer, I could hear his gentle voice saying to me, "Son, do
you have any idea where your Father has been lately?"

I remember coming home from the killing fields of Rwanda and
feeling a bit wounded by friends who seemed to have no interest in
trying to understand where I had been and what I had seen. I doubt
that I ever mentioned this to any of them. But I felt something of the
shallowness of some of my friendships when, coming back fresh from
an eyewitness experience of one of the most appalling events in human
history, they did not express even ten minutes of curiosity about what
I had seen. Given how unpleasant it all was, I really didn't blame them

for their lack of inquiry. In fact, most of the time I didn't like talking about it very much.

But those closest relatives and friends who really wanted to know me wouldn't let me get away with keeping the experience to myself. They wanted to understand where I had been, what I had seen and how I had been touched. They knew that they could never understand the deepest part of me if they didn't have some understanding of the hard things I had seen.

Likewise if we really want to know God, we should know something about where he has been—and what it has been like for him to suffer with all those who are hurting and abused. No one will ever *really* know what it was like for me to interview all those orphaned massacre survivors in Rwanda or to roll back a corpse in a Rwandan church and find the tiniest of skeletons under the remains of a mother who had tried to protect her baby with her own body. I would never expect people to totally understand. God doesn't expect this either. He knows that we can never comprehend the smallest fraction of the oppression and abuse that he has had to witness. But we can know him better if we try to understand something about his character and experience as the God of compassion—the God who suffers with the victims of injustice.

If nothing else, it will help us understand why the God of justice *hates* injustice and wants it to stop. If we had to see it and hear it every day like our God does, we would hate it too. To understand where the God of compassion has been is to begin to understand God's passion for justice. Justice, for our Lord and Savior Jesus Christ, is not a good idea, a noble aspiration, a theoretical satisfaction or an impersonal principle—it is his beating heart. He is the "man of sorrows, and familiar with suffering," who weeps with those who weep (Isaiah 53:3; John 11:33-35).

God's Boundless Compassion

God's compassion for the victims of injustice extends to all people, all around the world, without distinction or favor. When it comes to loving the people of the world, God suffers under none of our limitations. He doesn't feel so limited in his resources of compassion that he must establish boundaries for his caring or hierarchies of people, races, communities or nations to love. Rather, as the psalmist writes, "The LORD works righteousness and justice for *all* the oppressed" (Psalm 103:6). Indeed God seeks to establish justice "to save all the afflicted of the land" (Psalm 76:9).

The prophet Isaiah said that even the traditional enemy of Israel, the Egyptians, would one day cry out to God because of their oppression under foreign rulers, and he would hear their prayer: "It will be a sign and witness to the LORD Almighty in the land of Egypt. When they cry out to the LORD because of their oppressors, he will send them a savior and defender, and he will rescue them. So the LORD will make himself known to the Egyptians, and in that day they will acknowledge the LORD" (Isaiah 19:20-21). God never cuts himself off from those who cry to him in their suffering.

Claiming the Hope: Extending a Christlike Compassion

In my natural state my capacity for compassion and love begins with me and proceeds out (or not) to various concentric circles of human relationships with a decreasing fervency. I have a lot of compassion for my family, but by the time my compassion gets out to the remotest concentric circle where people in strange, faraway countries live, I usually don't have much left. Granted, this is quite understandable. The limitations of my mind, let alone the limitations of my heart, do not allow me to embrace everyone in the world in the same way that God does. It seems quite impossible for me to feel the same compassion for people with whom I share very little in common as I do for those with whom I share the same neighborhood, workplace, community, school or country.

While this is quite natural and quite human, it's not particularly godly. Of course, we will never manifest God's all-encompassing love for all people around the world, but the extent to which our compassion extends beyond our immediate circle is the extent to which we are loving more like God and less like our carnal selves. While we can never love the broad world as God does or even love our dearest loved one the way God does, we can at least agree on the ideal toward which we should seek to grow.

While it seems more natural to have compassion for those closest to us, we won't find in the Bible where Jesus asked us to have more compassion for our immediate neighbors or our compatriots than for anyone else. I believe he understands of our tendency to do so but is probably eager for us to reach out, as we are able (or as we seek his enabling), beyond our carnal limitations, prejudices, cultural mythologies and convenient stereotypes. Jesus calls us to be witnesses of his love, truth, salvation, compassion and justice "in Jerusalem [at home], and in all Judea and Samaria [nearby], and to the ends of the earth" (Acts 1:8).

Again this is the unique, biblical hope that Christians can offer to a world groaning under the heartache of injustice and oppression: God has compassion on the victims of injustice all over the world, among all people, without favor or distinction. We will, through our acts of compassion, give witness to our belief that what the Bible says is true, or not.

Six

Hope in the God of Moral Clarity

THE BIBLE TELLS US THAT THE GOD OF JUSTICE HAS COMpassion for the victims of injustice, and we find hope in this truth. The Bible also tells us how God regards the perpetrators of injustice, and in this there is hope as well. We do not have a God who cannot distinguish between justice and injustice. Rather, Scripture makes wonderfully and dreadfully clear that God judges and condemns those who perpetrate injustice. Quite simply, our holy God has a burning wrath for those who use their power and authority to take from those who are weak.

God's Severe Holiness

God's wrath is out of fashion. It's not something that we hear about, talk about or even think about. Like animal sacrifices, God's intense and severe anger toward sin strikes us as rather primitive—perhaps appropriate for dense, uncivilized, ancient peoples—something that God has gotten over. As J. I. Packer has observed, such a view probably comes from our habit of "following private religious hunches rather than learning about God from His own Word."[1]

If we truly want to know God, we must endeavor to understand the holy God who has made himself known in Scripture, the God who cannot accommodate himself to the sin of injustice, who can't get used to it, who continually suffers with those who are brutalized in body and spirit by the arrogance of humans. As J. I. Packer has again helpfully commented:

> No doubt it is true that the subject of divine wrath has in the past been handled speculatively, irreverently, even malevolently. No doubt there have been some who have preached of wrath and damnation with tearless eyes and no pain in their hearts. No doubt the sight of small sects cheerfully consigning the whole world, apart from themselves, to hell has disgusted many. Yet if we would know God, it is vital that we face the truth concerning his wrath, however unfashionable it may be, and however strong our initial prejudices against it. Otherwise we shall not understand the gospel of salvation from wrath, nor the propitiatory achievement of the cross, nor the wonder of the redeeming love of God. Nor shall we understand the hand of God in history.[2]

In fact, the knowledge of God's great anger toward and condemnation of injustice is what gives me hope to seek justice in this world. Standing with my boots deep in the reeking muck of a Rwandan mass grave where thousands of innocent people have been horribly slaughtered, I have no words, no meaning, no life, no hope if there is not a God of history and time who is absolutely outraged, absolutely furious, absolutely burning with anger toward those who took it into their own hands to commit such acts.

In honest humility I understand that as long as I am a member of the human race, I have within me the same base impulse of hatred and violence toward my neighbor, and that I also tremble as a sinner before a holy God. But it is in view of this severe holiness that I come to glimpse the awesome and mysterious mercy of a God who stands ready to forgive not only me, *but also* the genocidal killers of Rwanda.

A cheap forgiveness it is not, for it was purchased by God with the life of his own Son.

The Abuse of Power Is Sin

God's severe judgment flows out of his love for the victims of injustice and from the simple fact that injustice is sin. I, in my humanness, have a way of complicating injustice. I can talk about the abuse of power, especially by government officials, as politically immature, excessively authoritarian, bad policy, real politik and so on. But according to the Bible, God takes the abuse of power personally—and he calls it *sin.* As the prophet Amos declared to the elite of Israel who were abusing their power, "I know how many are your offenses and how great your sins. You oppress the righteous and take bribes and you deprive the poor of justice in the courts" (Amos 5:12).

With the possible exception of idolatry, we are hard pressed to find any other category of sin for which God's anger burns so bright. We are accustomed to hearing of God's hatred for idolatry, the very denial of who he is as God, but we may be surprised to find that God's hatred of injustice is every bit as passionate. The Bible teaches that everyone "who oppresses the poor shows contempt for their Maker" (Proverbs 14:31). The police officer who beats and robs the orphan, the corrupt official who forces little girls into prostitution, the jailer who tortures his detainee—all show contempt for or "insult" (NRSV) the very God of the universe who made the orphan, the little girl and the prisoner.

The prophet Ezekiel makes clear that those who worship idols and those who abuse their power to take from others call down on themselves the most severe holy anger.

There is a conspiracy of her *princes* within her like a roaring lion tearing its prey; they devour people, take treasures and precious things and make many widows within her. Her priests do violence to my law and profane my holy things; they do not distinguish between the holy and the common; they teach that there is no difference between the unclean and the clean; and they shut their eyes to the keeping of my Sabbaths, so that I am profaned among them. Her *officials* within her are like wolves tearing their prey; they shed blood and kill people to make unjust gain. Her prophets whitewash these deeds for them by false visions and lying divinations. They say, 'This is what the Sovereign LORD says'— when the LORD has not spoken. The people of the land practice extortion and commit robbery; they oppress the poor and needy and mistreat the alien, denying them justice.

"I looked for a man among them who would build up the wall and stand before me in the gap on behalf of the land so I would not have to destroy it, but I found none. So I will pour out my wrath on them and consume them with my fiery anger, bringing down on their own heads all they have done," declares the Sovereign LORD. (Ezekiel 22:25-31)

In this description of the grave sin of Israel, it is the people of public authority (the princes and officials) who are condemned by God for their abuse of power. They are described as wolves and lions—beings of great power—who have no moral excellence to direct their exercise of power. Rather, they simply tear at their prey for "unjust gain." They use their power to take from those who are weaker—to devour their lives, take their loved ones, plunder their treasure and precious possessions. Compounding this sin, the priests and religious officials do not use their influence to stand up for the poor and weak victims of injustice. Rather, they conspire with the oppressors, "whitewashing" their evil works, even dressing them up with false church talk about "the Lord" this and "the Lord" that.

Righteous Anger Against Injustice

God's response to such sin is not dispassionate. It is positively and fiercely angry.

We should not, of course, imagine God being angry like we are—irrational, disproportionate and rooted in fear. For unlike us he does not sin in his anger. But neither should we imagine that God shares our emotional casualness about the suffering of those who are brutalized by the abuse of power in our world. As we might feel about anyone who terrorized our child before our eyes, so we might imagine God's passionate response to those who abuse the people made in his image.

Of course, as Packer points out, God's response is unlike ours in that his indignation is always righteous, always judicial and always accompanied by an offer of redemption for the repentant.[3] But we would be off the mark if we ever got used to an image of God that did not respond to every injustice in our world with a passionate indignation. Such an image would be based on our private hunches about a God who looks like us rather than on what God has chosen to reveal about himself.

In a world despairing under the weight of those who use their power to take from those who are weak, we have a message of hope about the sovereign God of the universe who takes sides, who gets angry, who knows right from wrong.

> But your iniquities have separated you from your God; your sins have hidden his face from you, so that he will not hear. For your hands are stained with blood, your fingers with guilt. . . . The LORD looked and was displeased that there was no justice. He saw that there was no one, he was appalled that there was no one to intervene. (Isaiah 59:2, 16)

> "Their evil deeds have no limit; they do not plead the case of the fatherless to win it, they do not defend the rights of the poor. Should I not punish them for this?" declares the LORD. "Should

I not avenge myself on such a nation as this?" (Jeremiah 5:28-29)

This is what the LORD says: "Administer justice every morning; rescue from the hand of his oppressor the one who has been robbed, or my wrath will break out and burn like fire because of the evil you have done—burn with no one to quench it." (Jeremiah 21:12)

This is what the LORD says: "For three sins of Israel, even for four, I will not turn back my wrath. They sell the righteous for silver, and the needy for a pair of sandals. They trample on the heads of the poor as upon the dust of the ground and deny justice to the oppressed." (Amos 2:6-7)

This is what the LORD Almighty says: "Administer true justice; show mercy and compassion to one another. Do not oppress the widow or the fatherless, the alien or the poor. . . . " But they refused to pay attention. . . . So the LORD Almighty was very angry. (Zechariah 7:8-12)

Woe to you Pharisees, because you give God a tenth of your mint, rue and all other kinds of garden herbs, but you neglect justice and the love of God. You should have practiced the latter without leaving the former undone. (Luke 11:42)

Everywhere in the Bible, teachers—Jesus, Moses, King David, the prophets and the apostles—tell us that our God is a judge who knows right from wrong and is passionate about the difference.

Our postmodern mind is often uncomfortable with such a notion, and not without good reason. We have seen many pretenders to the throne of divine judgment—inquisitors, witch hunters, imperialists and self-righteous bigots who know nothing of the Lord in whose name they have so blithely gone about condemning, expelling and crushing other people. We are terrified to see what fallible, arrogant humanity can do with the hard steel of the absolute standards of right and wrong. In our revulsion we have lost our love for a perfect, righteous, divine judge who defends the weak, the voiceless and the oppressed with precisely that—an iron sword of truth and perfect moral clarity. As J. I. Packer noted, this adverse reaction to evil is what is necessary for moral perfection.

> The modern idea that a judge should be cold and dispassionate has no place in the Bible. The biblical judge is expected to love justice, play fair and loathe all ill-treatment of one person by another. An unjust judge, one who has no interest in seeing right triumph over wrong, is by biblical standards a monstrosity. The Bible leaves us in no doubt that God loves righteousness and hates iniquity.[4]

Claiming the Hope: Standing Fast with Moral Clarity

Let there be no mistake, evil and injustice thrive on moral ambiguity, equivocation, confusion and the failure to commit. Remembering that injustice is the abuse of *power,* we must know that injustice is strong, forceful, committed. In every case it will prevail against the uncertain, the unsure and the uncommitted.

As a boy I remember puzzling over a proverb of my football coach. He was teaching us how to tackle, and he told us that the best way to get hurt when tackling a big strong running back was to protect ourselves. In other words, our natural reaction to the sight of a huge, helmeted fullback barreling toward us was to act defensively, but this would end up getting us hurt. Rather than throwing our entire body into the tackle with as big a head of steam as we could muster, we instinctively wanted to slow down the combined velocity of the collision and to make what contact we could by grabbing with out-stretched arms.

Using such a cautious approach, we got slaughtered. Inevitably the tackler who tries slowing down gets run over, creamed, lunched. The running back knows where he is going—the end zone. At the first hint of a tackler's uncertainty, the running back knows that the best way to get there is by literally running through his opponent.

Oppressors also know where they are going, and they are committed. They know that feigning right and then feigning left can introduce moral uncertainty and that this puts them in a perfect position to run right over their opponents. The Nazis—the poster boys of evil—succeeded by moving about in a society paralyzed by a moral fog. It's hard to believe that anyone could be morally confused about the Nazis. But Dietrich Bonhoeffer, the great Lutheran minister who was hanged by Hitler's Gestapo for his failure to bow before Nazi idols, said that the failure of German Christians to resist the Nazi rise to power stemmed from their lack of moral clarity. "The great masquerade of evil," he wrote, "has played havoc with all our ethical concepts."[5]

At the point of moral challenge, Bonhoeffer said, the ones prepared to stand firm against injustice are those who put their trust in God, the righteous judge of moral truth: "Who stands fast? Only the man whose final standard is not his reason, his principles, his conscience, his freedom or his virtue, but who is ready to sacrifice all this when he is called to obedient and responsible action in faith and in exclusive allegiance to God—the responsible man who tries to make his whole life an answer to the question and call of God."[6]

Here then is our hope. In a world where oppressors stand ready to exploit every moral hesitation, equivocation and complexity, we serve a God who responds to injustice with a blazing moral clarity and passionate commitment to what is right. In studying Scripture we can recover the hope and beauty of a holy judge who stands four-square with the victims of injustice.

Seven

Hope in the God of Rescue

An Action Plan

T HE MISSIONARIES AND CHRISTIAN SERVICE WORKERS churches support around the world see some awful injustice in the communities where they serve. At the International Justice Mission we hear about it and see it when we meet with them.

Rescuing Rosa

Not long ago I was in one of Manila's poorest neighborhoods meeting with the director of a center for abused and abandoned girls—a ministry supported by the Christian and Missionary Alliance Church. The director, a gentle Filipino woman in her late forties named Maria, gave me a tour of their small but clean and bright facility and introduced me to some of the thirty orphans and abused runaways who had found the shelter of Jesus' embrace within the center's walls.

Maria and Agatha, a social worker at the center, began to tell me the girls' stories. Agatha left the room to get some papers and came back to tell me about a girl named Rosa. Just thirteen years old herself, Rosa had given birth to a child a few months before. They let me hold the tiny, precious baby. Her name was May. According to Maria, when Rosa was only twelve, a man in the neighborhood raped her, and May was the child born from that rape. Worse, said Agatha, almost a year later, the man still walks the streets. Agatha sees the alleged rapist in her neighborhood when he stays with his girlfriend down the street.

"Did anyone report the crime?" I asked. "Oh yes," said Agatha and Maria, handing me the documents from the local court demonstrating that a proper complaint had been filed. The local prosecutor's preliminary hearing had led him to seek an arrest warrant from the court. In the file was the warrant—an order from the regional trial court ordering local law-enforcement officials to immediately arrest Rosa's alleged assailant. But as Maria, Agatha, Rosa and all the other girls at the center knew, the man still freely walked the streets. Officials had made no effort to arrest him, apparently because he was a family friend of the local police.

Maria and Agatha had pleaded with the police, and they even contacted the National Bureau of Investigation (the Filipino FBI) for help. But days went by, weeks, then months, and nothing ever happened.

By the time I arrived at the center, Maria and Agatha had lost any hope of securing justice and lasting protection for Rosa. All the laws in the world will do no good if no one enforces them, and in this poor neighborhood in Manila there was no one to enforce the law for a girl like Rosa.

Under such circumstances, where can Rosa, Maria and Agatha find hope? What hope does God offer in his Word?

God's Affirmation of Action

As we have seen, God makes three clear affirmations about himself in regard to injustices like this. First, he affirms that in Rosa's struggle for justice he stands on her side. He declares himself to be a God of justice who hates the way this man has used his superior physical power, not to protect a vulnerable girl but to take from her what personal dignity and sanctity she had. Second, God affirms his compassion for her; he has suffered through this brutal injustice with her, he has heard her cry and sees her suffering. Third, God affirms that he condemns with holy anger this nightmarish act that has been perpetrated against her and that he is prepared in perfect righteousness to punish her assailant for such an act.

God also makes a fourth affirmation: he seeks active rescue for victims of injustice like Rosa. God not only stands at Rosa's side, suffers with her and condemns the assault, he also deeply desires that her assailant be brought to justice and that she be protected from such abuse.

According to Scripture, God's justice, compassion and righteousness move him to an active, real-world response. This is not a God who offers sympathy, best wishes or cruel character-building exercises. This is a God who wants evildoers brought to account and vulnerable people protected—here and now!

> Why does the wicked man revile God?
>   Why does he say to himself,
>   "He won't call me to account"?
> But you, O God, do see trouble and grief;
>   you consider it to take it in hand.
> The victim commits himself to you;
>   you are the helper of the fatherless.
> Break the arm of the wicked and evil man;
>   call him to account for his wickedness
>   that would not be found out.
> The LORD is King for ever and ever;
>   the nations will perish from his land.
> You hear, O LORD, the desire of the afflicted;
>   you encourage them, and you listen to their cry,

defending the fatherless and the oppressed,
   in order that man, who is of the earth,
   may terrify no more. (Psalm 10:13-18)

God doesn't glibly spiritualize the suffering of injustice, for he himself has endured it. He knows that the lash is real, that the fist hurts, that torture kills and that injustice can so brutalize our spirit as to make us feel forsaken by the heavenly Father. God knows that, ultimately, lost souls need a Savior and that "our struggle is not against flesh and blood, but against the rulers, against the authorities, against the powers of this dark world and against the spiritual forces of evil in the heavenly realms" (Ephesians 6:12). But he also clearly knows that the powers of darkness and forces of evil can manifest themselves on this earth as real hunger, real nakedness, real imprisonment, real beatings and real injustice. And while never neglecting or subordinating spiritual needs, Jesus called his followers to respond to hunger with food, to nakedness with clothes, to imprisonment with visitation, to beatings with bandages and to injustice with justice (Matthew 15:32-38; 25:35-36; Luke 10:34; 11:42). As the apostle James wrote, "Suppose a brother or sister is without clothes and daily food. If one of you says to him, 'Go, I wish you well; keep warm and well fed,' but does nothing about his physical needs, what good is it?" (James 2:15-16).

Accordingly, our God seeks active rescue for the victims of oppression:

My whole being will exclaim,
   "Who is like you, O LORD?
You rescue the poor from those too strong for them,
   the poor and needy from those who rob them." (Psalm 35:10)

I know that the LORD secures justice for the poor and upholds the cause of the needy. (Psalm 140:12)

Sing to the LORD! Give praise to the LORD! He rescues the life
of the needy from the hands of the wicked. (Jeremiah 20:13)

The Spirit of the Lord is on me, because he has anointed me . . .
to release the oppressed. (Luke 4:18)

This is good news! This is the armor of hope that allows us to do
battle in an ugly world of injustice. From God's holy Word we come
armed with four powerful affirmations: God is on the side of justice.
God sees and cares. God condemns injustice. God seeks rescue for the
victims.

How Does God Seek Justice?

But sitting in Maria's office, holding May in my arms and handing
Agatha back her worthless arrest warrant, all of this nice theology
meets the real world. It is wonderful to know that God is on Rosa's
side, that he cares for her, that he condemns such an assault and that
he actively seeks to "secure justice for the poor and to uphold the cause
of the needy." But Rosa's alleged rapist is being protected by corrupt
local officials.

So Rosa could ask a perfectly legitimate question: If God seeks
justice for the oppressed, *how* exactly does he do that? If, as Psalm 10
says, God helps the fatherless, defends the oppressed, "breaks the
arm" of evil people and calls them to account for their wickedness—
how does he do this? How is he going to do this for Rosa?

A fair question. Do we have an answer? I think we do, and it has
everything to do with you and me.

Unless the work of seeking justice is a category of endeavor that is
completely different from every other activity on earth that is important
to God, the answer to the how question has something to do with what
God's people do or don't do. If you think about it, two truths apply to
everything that God wants accomplished on earth: (1) he could accomplish it on his own through supernatural power; but instead, (2) he

chooses for the most part to limit himself to accomplishing that which he can achieve through the obedience of his people.

God desires that the gospel of Jesus Christ be proclaimed throughout the earth, and he could accomplish this quite swiftly with an overwhelming trumpet blast from heaven that would leave no doubt about who is Lord. And yet God calls his people to be his ambassadors, to proclaim his good news to the nations. As Paul asked, "How, then, can they call on the one they have not believed in? And how can they believe in the one of whom they have not heard? And how can they hear without someone preaching to them?" (Romans 10:14). Of course, the cheeky answer would be to say, "Well, God could tell them directly." But clearly God has chosen a different plan. By some great mystery and enormous privilege, he has chosen to use his people, empowered by his Spirit, to complete this task. He simply does not have another plan. Indeed, "how beautiful are the feet of those who brings good news!" (Romans 10:15).

The same principle applies to healing the sick, feeding the hungry, clothing the destitute, sheltering the homeless. Through supernatural intervention God could meet all of these needs, yet he has given these tasks to his people. He gives us the great honor and privilege of being his instruments. In response to God's call Christian ministries like Compassion International, World Relief, and World Vision have fed millions of hungry children. Christian medical missions have brought sight to the blind and life to the dying all around the world. In the name of Christ, Habitat for Humanity has brought shelter to thousands of families across the globe. The Salvation Army has shared warm coats and the love of Christ with countless men and women shivering in the cold.

How does God proclaim the gospel and work on behalf of those in need? Clearly, he does it through the obedience of his people. True, he has established economies and a fruitful earth to provide for the needs of humankind, and he has created natural physiological proc-

esses for healing the body. But when these fail and our neighbor stands
before us hungry, sick, naked and vulnerable to the elements, through
whose hands does God reach out to meet their needs and show his
love? Ours. We are God's hands of mercy and love. Occasions certainly may arise when God intervenes in some utterly supernatural
fashion that bypasses all human instruments, but overwhelmingly God
chooses to limit himself to those miracles he can perform through
people who are obedient to his call.

So it is with justice. When governments and those whom God
has placed in authority fail to protect those who are weak, God
looks to his people to be his voice of judgment and his hands of
rescue. "So justice is driven back, and righteousness stands at a
distance; truth has stumbled in the streets, honesty cannot enter.
Truth is nowhere to be found, and whoever shuns evil becomes a
prey. The LORD looked and was displeased that there was no justice.
He saw that there was no one, he was appalled that there was no
one to intervene" (Isaiah 59:14-16).

God declared to his people, "Is not this the kind of fasting I have
chosen: to loose the chains of injustice and untie the cords of the yoke,
to set the oppressed free and break every yoke?" (Isaiah 58:6).

Who Will Seek God's Justice?

In the twentieth century Christians were quick to understand the
ministry God called us to in preaching the gospel. In recent years we
have begun to understand that we are to be God's hands in feeding the
hungry, healing the sick and sheltering the homeless. But how many
of us have thought that when it comes to seeking justice, rescuing the
oppressed, defending the orphan and pleading for the widow, God
must have some other plan, some other strategy that doesn't depend
on his people?

As a million Christian Promise Keepers gathered in Washington,
D.C., under the banner of "Standing in the Gap," I wondered how

many of us had ever read the context in Ezekiel from which the phrase comes. The passage refers to God's search for a righteous witness amid the brutal abuse of power by government officials (covered up by corrupt religious authorities).

> Her [Jerusalem's] princes . . . devour people, take treasures and precious things and make many widows. . . . Her officials . . . shed blood and kill people to make unjust gain. . . . The people of the land practice extortion and commit robbery; they oppress the poor and needy and mistreat the alien, denying them justice. "I looked for a man among them who would build up the wall and stand before me in the gap on behalf of the land so I would not have to destroy it, but I found none." (Ezekiel 22:25-30)

No thoughtful Christian would say, "Sure Jesus wants his gospel preached, the hungry fed, the sick healed and the naked clothed, but that doesn't have anything to do with me." And yet many of us have been content to praise God as the God of justice, to extol his compassion for the weak and voiceless and to declare his promises to "rescue the life of the needy from the hands of the wicked"—all the while harboring a suspicion that God generally accomplishes these miracles with mysterious winds or vague, magical forces of history (Jeremiah 20:13). Worse, viewing a world of injustice from a seat in the grandstand, we may be tempted to shake our fist at God, demanding to know why he's not harder at work blowing those mysterious winds or moving those magical vague forces of history. Like the Israelites we often weary God with our words, saying, "Where is the God of justice?" (Malachi 2:17).

Meanwhile the Spirit of God stands on the playing field of history saying, "I looked for a person among them, but I found none." To paraphrase Isaiah, "The LORD looked and was displeased that Rosa received no justice. He was appalled that there was no one to intervene" (Isaiah 59:15-16).

There is no question that God grants justice. As Jesus put it, "he will *quickly* grant justice" (Luke 18:8 NRSV) The question is, Will God find faith on the earth? Will he find his instruments of mercy and justice, his people, ready for service (Luke 18:1-8)?

Over time I have come to see questions about suffering in the world not so much as questions of God's character but as questions about the obedience and faith of God's people. Given the painful injustice that Rosa continues to endure, it is no wonder that she may be tempted to despair as the psalmist did: "Why, O LORD, do you stand far off? Why do you hide yourself in time of trouble?" (Psalm 10:1). But gradually it has occurred to me that the problem may not be that God is so far off; the problem may be that *God's people* are far off.

Working Miracles with God

A preacher once asked me (and the rest of his congregation) to consider a scene that has stayed with me ever since. He asked us to recall the story about the feeding of the five thousand. The disciples brought complaints about the hungry multitude to Jesus, and he responded compassionately by blessing the bits of food from a boy's lunch—five loaves of bread and two fishes. "Then he gave them to the disciples, and the disciples gave them to the people. They ate and all were satisfied" (Matthew 14:19). The speaker then asked us to imagine a scenario in which the disciples just kept thanking Jesus for all the bread and fish—without passing them along to the people. He asked us to imagine the disciples starting to be overwhelmed by the piles of multiplying loaves and fish surrounding them, yelling out to Jesus, "Thank you, thank you, thank you, thank you, thank you, thank you, thank you, thank you!"—all the while never passing along the food to people. And then beneath the mounting piles of food, the disciples even could be heard complaining to Jesus that he wasn't doing anything about the hungry multitude.

This simple illustration struck my heart deeply. How kind of Jesus to include the boy and the disciples in his miracle. Surely he could have done it differently. Surely he could have commanded the heavens to unload manna and quail right on top of everybody. But how beautifully he included the boy's tiny offering. Jesus (the Creator of all things, seen and unseen) no more needed those five loaves and two fish than my wife and I need our three-year-old's "help" in baking cinnamon rolls for visitors. But what a wonderful, life-changing day for that boy to be part of Jesus' miracle. How fun for the disciples to go among the grateful, joyful multitudes—to be the hands dispensing Christ's supernatural power and love. How ridiculous, on the other hand, that they should imagine that the vast piles of bread and fish should be given to them for any other reason than to feed those who were in need.

So too with the ministry of God's rescue for the oppressed in the world. *How* does God rescue the life of the needy from the hands of the wicked? Overwhelmingly, he does it through those who choose to follow him in faith and obedience. He doesn't need our "help," but he chooses to use us.

Looking at the millions of bonded child laborers in India or the thousands of child prostitutes in Asia or thousands of torture victims twisting and bleeding in the world's forgotten jail cells, we can say to God, "Thank you, thank you, thank you, thank you, thank you, thank you, thank you, thank you! Thank you for all the power, protection, freedom and justice you have granted us in sparing us from such fates. Thank you, thank you, thank you, thank you, thank you, thank you, thank you, thank you!"

Or we can ask, "What have you given me, Father, that I might help those who don't have power, who don't have protection, who don't have freedom, who don't have justice?"

God's Plan of Action
This then is the earth-shattering truth with which God yearns to renew

our minds and change the lives of those who suffer: The almighty God of the universe is prepared to use *us,* his people, to seek justice, to rescue the oppressed, to defend the orphan and to plead for the widow. Concretely, he is prepared to use you and me to protect Rosa and others and to bring their oppressors to justice.

How? By using the gifts, resources, relationships, expertise and power that he has given us. Because the reason he has granted us these things is not merely for our joy (though great joy they rightly bring) but so that we might serve those who lack them.

How does God vindicate Rosa's cause? In her particular case God was prepared to use some of us at the International Justice Mission.

God's Justice Prevails

When Maria, the director of a Christian center for abused and abandoned girls, referred the case to us, their sense of hopelessness was overwhelming. They had done everything they were supposed to do. They had gone through the trauma and humiliation of filing formal charges. Rosa and the eyewitness had given sworn statements. They had obtained a warrant of arrest for the rapist. They had pleaded with the local police to execute the warrant of arrest. They had even contacted a member of the National Bureau of Investigation to make inquires on their behalf. All to no avail.

When I met Maria at the center to hear their story, more than three months had passed since the court issued its warrant of arrest. Maria and Agatha had come to understand that the assailant was a family friend of powerful local officials and that by comparison they were nobodies.

There I sat, with the nobodies, holding a fading copy of an arrest warrant. But now I could see, really see, what the Bible was talking about. The mandate was always there, but the words had seemed vague and theoretical: "Seek justice, rescue the oppressed, defend the orphan, plead for the widow." Now they spoke very directly, very specifically to me: "Seek justice for Rosa. Rescue Rosa. Defend Rosa. Plead for Rosa."

Given our background, my colleagues and I knew how to do this. We tracked down her assailant and found out where he was hanging out. We got a photo of him and blew it up into a wanted poster. We obtained copies of the arrest warrant, the preliminary investigation by the prosecutor, the sworn statements and other relevant case documents. A Christian lawyer in Washington, D.C., volunteered his time to package all the materials properly and sent it directly to the commander of the Philippine National Police and to the specific woman judge who had ordered the arrest of the alleged rapist. Three hours after the national police commander received our package, Rosa's alleged assailant was arrested and behind bars.

Maria faxed to our offices a copy of the local newspaper with its banner headline: "International Letter Leads to Arrest of Rape Suspect." The article described the events of the past few months, concluding that Rosa and those who cared for her "must have surely heaved a sigh of relief, half-thankful that the suspect has been finally arrested. But were it not for a letter from abroad, they may not have anything to be thankful for at all."

We were elated, and we praised and thanked God for his faithfulness in answering our prayers and the prayers of the people at the center. It was awesome to pause for a moment and consider that God had answered those prayers, not through mysterious winds or forces of history but through us. He didn't *need* us, and the steps we actually took were rather elemental. But we were truly, tangibly the hands of God Almighty, the God of justice, as he expressed his compassion and love to Rosa. What an honor! What a privilege!

Three Promises of God

Through this one small story we can see three promises of God on which we base all our hope for bringing about justice: (1) Ours is a God of justice, a God who hates injustice and wants it to stop; (2) God desires to use his people as his instruments for seeking justice and rescuing the oppressed; and (3) God does not give his people a ministry that he won't empower.

Like you, perhaps, I am encouraged by the first promise—the knowledge that God is a God of justice. But frankly, when I look at the brutal and pervasive injustice in our world, the second promise—that he is prepared to use me to seek justice—strikes me as rather overwhelming. Perhaps it does for you as well. But then I consider this third promise, and it changes everything. *God does not call us to a ministry that he will not empower.* Period. And here is where we find real hope.

How pathetic it would be if God said, "Seek justice, rescue the oppressed, defend the orphan and plead for the widow—and good luck to you out there!" But sometimes we act as if that's precisely the way he works, suspecting that he calls us to a grand, godly, utterly impossible work in the world and then doesn't bother to show up. But of course this is not true. As John Perkins explained at a justice forum sponsored by the International Justice Mission, Jesus promised that when he left the Holy Spirit would come and we would receive "power" to be his witnesses—witnesses to his gospel, his love, his mercy and his justice (Acts 1:8).

The Joy in Doing Justice

Acting by God's empowerment doesn't mean that we will always be safe, that we will find the tasks before us easy or that we will triumph in ways we can always understand or measure. But from the bottom of my soul I believe that God has indescribable mysteries and miracles stored up for his people who seek justice in his name—miracles of a kind and quality that Western Christians, anyway, have not experienced in generations. Truly, "No eye has seen, no ear has heard, no mind has conceived what God has prepared for those who love him" (1 Corinthians 2:9). I believe that God is prepared to show his faithfulness as the God of justice—through his people and to his own glory—in ways that perhaps only Esther and Gideon could begin to understand.

We will not see heaven come to earth or the world purged of injustice. But we will see the God of justice being faithful. We will see him "rescue the poor from those too strong for them" (Psalm 35:10). We will see that he "secures justice for the poor and upholds the cause of the needy" (Psalm 140:12-13). If we simply and courageously make ourselves available to him, Jesus Christ himself will "release the oppressed" (Luke 4:18)—and we will know the extraordinary joy of watching him do it *through us.*

We will meet with risks and defeats and disappointments, and we will see how deeply fallen the world truly is. We will be "hard pressed on every side, but not crushed; perplexed, but not in despair; persecuted, but not abandoned; struck down, but not destroyed" (2 Corinthians 4:7-9).

In meeting with difficulties, we simply claim our God, the name of Jesus Christ and the truth of the holy Scriptures. "For the eyes of the Lord are on the righteous and his ears are attentive to their prayer, but the face of the Lord is against those who do evil. Who is going to harm you if you are eager to do good? But even if you should suffer for what is right, you are blessed" (1 Peter 3:12-14).

Part 3

Real-World Tools for Rescuing the Oppressed

Eight

Answers for Difficult Questions

God & Injustice

VULNERABILITY IN THE FACE OF AN ABUSIVE OPPRESSOR occurs with different people in different ways every day—all around the world. The reality of these injustices poses some fundamental questions for those who claim to trust in the God of justice revealed in Scripture.

Why Do Such Injustices Happen?

The first question we may ask is, *Why do massacres and other atrocities like Rosa's rape occur?* On one level this is the easiest question to answer.

I don't mean to be glib in stating this so simply, but I believe the reason these offenses occur is because people choose to indulge their selfish and brutal urges to dominate the defenseless. They have chosen to live in rebellion against the God of love and goodness who made them, and now they are left with nothing but their own sinful nature, or whatever you want to call it—the unrestrained will to power, the unmediated libido, the nausea of existence, misogynistic male aggression. Scripture graphically describes such people: "Their throats are open graves; their tongues practice deceit. . . . Their feet are swift to shed blood; ruin and misery mark their ways, and the way of peace they do not know. There is no fear of God before their eyes" (Romans 3:10-18).

If people have no respect for God, no love for their Maker, I would ask the question the another way: Why *not* pillage, rape, persecute and murder? If it feels good, and they can get away with it, why not? If God is dead or does not exist, as these people believe, why are not all things permitted? Why should they restrain themselves? Because it's *just wrong?* Because it's *not the way civilized people behave?* Because *what goes around comes around?* Because *they'll end up feeling terrible inside?*

Within tidy circles of properly socialized and reasonable people, such appeals can seem like they actually have the power to restrain people from doing what they otherwise feel like doing. But in the real world outside the philosophy seminar room, oppressors frankly don't care that you think it's *just wrong.* Who are *you,* they ask, to foist your random moral intuition on them? Who are *you* to tell them or the lords of the Third Reich what civilized people should and should not do? If what goes around tends to come around, then there's no moral problem, only a practical problem of making sure it doesn't come around to you. They think, *Fine, if being brutal makes you feel terrible inside, then don't do it. But it makes me feel powerful, alive, exhilarated and masterful, so quit whining—unless you want to try to stop me.*

This description of a dark Nietzschean world of self-will—a vacuum devoid of moral authority or spiritual resources for good—used to seem excessively melodramatic to me. But then I got out more. The world is truly full of brutal oppression because humans have rejected their Maker, the source of all goodness, mercy, compassion, truth, justice and love.

Personally, I do not have a difficult time understanding that without

God I am as lost as the oppressor. When I don't depend on the Holy Spirit moment by moment every day, I see the ugliness in me come out: selfishness, pride, insensitivity, anger, gossip, ingratitude, self-righteousness, self-deception, jealousy and covetousness, to name a few.

For most of us these latent forces of great sin are kept in check by various social and cultural restraints, but we should be under no illusions about what exists at the human core. Perfectly *ordinary* human beings are actually capable of being mass murderers. In Rwanda (to say nothing of Eastern Europe during the Holocaust), the killing was not performed by specially trained pathological killers but by ordinary people. When all restraints are released, farmers, clerks, school principals, mothers, doctors, mayors and carpenters can pick up machetes and hack to death defenseless women and children. And this happened in a nation where 80 percent of the citizens identified themselves as Christian. Unless we wish to cling to racist theories about Africans, or mythologies of education or civilization (as in Germany in 1933), we must face the objective, historical facts of the matter. The person without God (or perhaps worse, the person without God but claiming "God," "Jesus," "Muhammad," whatever) is a very scary creature.

As a columnist for the *Washington Post* recently asked about the massacres in Algeria, where an eight-year-old boy was nearly decapitated while having his throat slit,

> What could an 8-year-old have done to warrant such a death? What could have been his crime, his ideology, his belief, his threat—and his threat to whom? What explains the murder of a child? Whatever the answer, it must be applied over and over again. The killing of children is an Algerian staple. In some villages, they have been hurled against walls. So, too, is the killing of the women and the aged—and, of course, of men. These people don't seem to be politically involved; nor are they members of the military or police. They are nothing more than peasants and yet they have

been murdered by the thousands, often in ways so gruesome as to be incomprehensible. In the first week of January [1998], as many as 1,000 people were killed in villages about 150 miles from Algiers. The savagery is such that you cannot believe human beings—as opposed to animals—are responsible.[1]

Dostoyevsky would argue that the columnist insults animals when characterizing the work of unrestrained human nature as animal-like. In *The Brothers Karamazov,* the brother Ivan comments on the alleged atrocities of the Turks and Circassians

> who, fearing a general uprising of the Slav population, set villages afire, rape women and children, nail their prisoners to fences by their ears and leave them in that state until morning, when they hang them, and commit other atrocities that are hard to imagine. People often describe such human cruelty as "bestial," but that's, of course, unfair to animals, for no beast could ever be as cruel as man, I mean as refinedly and artistically cruel. The tiger simply gnaws and tears his victim to pieces because that's all he knows. It would never occur to a tiger to nail people to fences by their ears, even if he were able to do it.[2]

These are dark discourses on our underlying nature, but at the bottom of this black well is the answer to our hard question about why people like Rosa are oppressed—enslaved, raped, tortured, killed— and why they find no justice. In truth we live in an exceedingly dangerous world in rebellion against its Maker, a world filled with prideful, frightened, willful, violent people who have incrementally chosen to cut themselves off from the Creator's goodness, love, mercy and justice. As C. S. Lewis sums it up, this is the Fall of humanity: "Man is now a horror to God and himself and a creature ill-adapted to the universe not because God made him so but because he has made himself so by the abuse of his free will."[3]

Why Does God Allow Injustice?

Of course, this answer readily begs another infinitely more difficult question: *Why does God allow humans to so abuse their free will?* Why might God permit someone to hack another human to death? Why does God allow so much injustice in the world?

I believe I've heard most of the neat answers to these questions—a set of answers which in Christian circles often explode in a discussion like an emergency ejection seat, rescuing relieved passengers from a crash-and-burn confrontation with unpleasant mysteries. Frankly, the pat answers don't work, and the insensitivity that I have seen in myself and in others as we have addressed ourselves to Rosa's and others' pain has bordered at times on cruelty. Let's be honest. This is hard. As Irving Greenberg, a writer on the Holocaust, has said, "No statement, theological or otherwise, should be made that would not be credible in the presence of burning children."[4]

We must not be afraid, however, to descend all the way down into the dark well of truth until we find its hard bottom. For there in the dark bedrock, standing ankle deep in muck, we will nevertheless find hard stone underneath our feet—our first immovable foothold for the climb out. Our climb will not take us soaring into the heavens but may be just enough to get us out of the black well, up onto the ground, where we can walk to that place where God is calling us. As we climb, the Scriptures urge us to look for the footholds of humility, the cross, love and eternity.

Foothold 1: We Start with Humility

The wisest and deepest Christian response to the question of why God permits such injustice has always begun with humility. Fifteen hundred years ago Salvian the Presbyter, one of the great fathers of the early church, confronted the question squarely and honestly: "Why does the whole world fall prey to powers for the most part unjust? Perhaps a rational and fairly consistent answer would be: 'I do not know.' For I do not know the secrets of God. . . . I am a man; I do not understand the secrets of God."[5] Job learned firsthand that for people to speak of the first order motivation or design of the Almighty Creator God is to speak of what they don't understand, "things too wonderful" to know (Job 42:3). In the face of injustice we cannot presume to speak for God beyond that which he has revealed about himself, for even that which we know from God we know only "in part" (1 Corinthians 13:9).

Foothold 2: We Remember the Cross

Of course, this notion of a lofty, unknowable God who sits beyond the reach of my objections strikes me as infuriating. In the context of human suffering like Rosa's, I find no love for a God who sits on some serene, detached cloud of mystery rolling his eyes and exchanging if-they-only-knew smirks with the angels.

But then I remember Jesus, and I recall what my God, the one true God, is really like—the God of the cross. Even in the midst of the deepest human anguish, I remember why it is that I love Jesus and trust what he says. John Stott expresses my own convictions most beautifully:

> I could never myself believe in a God, if it were not for the cross. The only God I believe in is the One Nietzsche ridiculed as "God on the cross." In a real world of pain, how could one worship a God who was immune to it? I have entered many Buddhist temples in different Asian countries and stood respectfully before the statue of the Buddha, his legs crossed, arms folded, eyes closed, the ghost of a smile playing round his mouth, a remote look on his face, detached from the agonies of the world. But each time after a while I have had to turn away. And in imagination I have turned instead to that lonely, twisted tortured figure on the cross, nails through hands and feet, back lacerated, limbs

wrenched, brow bleeding from thorn pricks, mouth dry and intolerably thirsty, plunged in God-forsaken darkness. That is the God for me! He laid aside his immunity to pain. He entered into our world of flesh and blood, tears and death. He suffered for us. Our suffering became more manageable in light of his. There is still a question mark against human suffering, but over it we boldly stamp another mark, the cross which symbolizes divine suffering. "The cross of Christ . . . is God's only self-justification in a world such as ours."[6]

So when at times I flippantly challenge the Almighty as to why he allows horrendous suffering, I am pulled up in a shudder of humility as I recall that there is no measure of his creation's suffering that he has not been willing to bear himself. Indeed, I stand before a God whose thoughts—and sufferings—are too great for me.

Nevertheless, in all reverence it is right to ask, What, if anything, has God revealed about why he allows evil people to abuse those who are weak?

Foothold 3: We Recognize That God Desires Our Love, Freely Given

What we know "in part" is that in creating humankind, God would be satisfied with nothing less than a deep relationship of authentic love with each man and woman. He wants us to know the glory of being loved by him. He wants us to experience the glory of knowing him—*truly* knowing him. He wants us to experience the wonder of returning passionate, exultant, personal love to the Maker of the universe, the lover of our souls. The nature of such a relationship, however, requires that he also make us free *not* to love him, free *not* to know him—free to *reject* him and his Spirit.

Consequently, the unfathomable dignity which God has bestowed on each man and woman, the resplendent magnificence with which

God exalted those whom he had made in his own image, requires that they be free to turn their backs on him. And as they have done so, all people, to varying degrees, have made themselves a horror—to themselves and to their fellow humans—redeemable only by the ultimate sacrifice of their Maker.

Looking at the human carnage and suffering wreaked by humanity's rebellion against God, we might think that God paid us an "intolerable compliment" in bestowing this "terrible gift of freedom."[7] We might argue with God as Dostoyevsky's Grand Inquisitor argued with Jesus: "You wanted their freely given love rather than the servile rapture of slaves subdued forever by a display of power. And, here again, you overestimated men."[8] But in contending so with God we must be aware that we are arguing about the ultimate value of his yearning to truly and deeply love us and to be loved by us—and we are doing so without the benefit of eternity. It's somewhat like arguing whether it's worthwhile to go see the Grand Canyon based on what one has seen of a drainage ditch in one's yard.

Foothold 4: We Embrace the Hope of Eternity

I do not lightly invoke eternity as a foothold for climbing out of our paralyzing question about why God allows injustice, but as a convinced Christian, invoke it I must. I believe I have seen, more than most, something of the magnitude and depth of the pain endured by the innocent of this earth. I have stood within the walls of a Rwandan church piled knee high with slaughtered innocence, evidence all around of the unanswered cries for mercy they raised to God and humankind. And I can honestly say that, this side of eternity, I walk away from such a sight with no meaning, no hope, no reason for going on. No words—at all.

But Jesus, whom I have come to trust and respect, asks me to understand that eternity changes everything. He asks me to conceive of a world outside of time where even those who have lost brothers or sisters or mother or father or children will receive back a hundred times as much in the life eternal (Matthew 19:29). He asks me to try and picture a world beyond the present so glorious in its beauty, goodness and rightness that I should "leap for joy" (his words, not mine) when I suffer the hatred, exclusion, insults and rejection that accompany the path to such a place (Luke 6:22-23).

According to the apostle Paul, "Our present sufferings are not worth comparing with the glory that will be revealed in us" (Romans 8:18). Such a dismissive attitude toward earthly suffering might ring hollow from most people. But I would leave it to more hearty souls to challenge the credibility of a man who had not only been granted a peek at the world to come but in this world had been flogged five times with thirty-nine lashes, beaten three times with rods, nearly stoned to death, and imprisoned falsely more times than one could count (2 Corinthians 11:23-28; 12:3-4).

I have every sympathy for those who look into Rosa's eyes or at the lifeless forms piled up in Rwanda and say that nothing in the next world can compensate for the hurt. But I don't honestly know that that's the case.

One could say that the notion of eternity is just pie in the sky, but as C. S. Lewis observed, either there is pie in the sky or there is not.[9] The Scripture's claims about the consolation of eternity are either true or not. Either death will be a black, mocking insult to the injury of life, or we will hear "a loud voice from the throne saying, 'Now the dwelling of God is with men, and he will live with them. They will be his people, and God himself will be with them and be their God. He will wipe every tear from their eyes. There will be no more death or mourning or crying or pain, for the old order of things has passed away . . . I am making everything new!' " (Revelation 21:3-5).

If such claims are true, it just might change everything. If there were no pie in the sky, Jesus said, "I would have told you" (John 14:2). But if Jesus does not rightly claim absolute divine authority for such statements, then not only is he not a good teacher, he is a cruel liar or a delusional psychopath of the first order. Moreover, if there is no pie in the sky, I frankly don't have any earthly hope that is not immediately crushed under the weight of the empirical data of despair around me.

The pie in the sky is not, for me, a reason to escape from the needs of our world; rather, it offers the nourishment of spirit that has empowered Christians through the ages to serve those needs tirelessly, even unto death.

In the months after I returned from Rwanda, every time I entered a church service I found my mind subconsciously driven to horrible calculations about what it would take, and how long it would take, to murder the entire congregation with machetes—as it happened in scores of churches across Rwanda. I hated thinking it, but there it was. Every time this left me looking to the ceiling, trying to blink back the welling tears so they would not stream down my face. The image of the broken waste of all those Rwandan women and children would overwhelm me, and yet, through nearly clenched teeth I would find my inner soul testify in the words of a hymn that would not stay down: "Crown him the Lord of life / Who triumphed o'er the grave / Who rose victorious to the strife / for those he came to save / His glories now we sing / Who died and rose on high / Who died eternal life to bring / And lives that death may die."[10]

By the grace of God I believe this testimony is true. Somehow, I find the hope of eternity "trustworthy and true" (Revelation 21:5).

When falling into the well of doubt about why God permits injustice on the earth, I scrape my way out by standing first on the limits of my human knowledge. I grab on to the character of the compassionate Creator revealed on the cross. I step up to the mysterious foothold offered by the terrible gift of free will, and lunge up to the dusty ground onto the hope of eternity.

Brushing myself off, I finally get to my feet and face the task before me—preparing my mind and heart to help those like Rosa who suffer because of injustice.

Nine

Anatomy of Injustice

Coercion & Deception

W E MAY HAVE EXPERIENCED OCCASIONS WHEN WE FEEL the Spirit of God stirring our heart to help those who suffer under oppression, but then we immediately feel the undertow of very practical questions. What exactly can we do? How can we actually make a difference? What practical steps are we supposed to take?

These questions leap from our hearts with eagerness, but they most often limp back to us so devoid of practical answers that the inspiration is almost impossible to sustain. Over time a suspicion takes root that incidents of injustice in our world are actually more akin to natural disasters—tragic and sad, but not something we can do much about.

G. K. Chesterton once wrote that "the Christian ideal has not been tried and found wanting; it has been found difficult and left untried."[1] Something similar could be said about the biblical call to seek justice in the world. It's not so much that we have vigorously pursued the call and found God unfaithful in his promises but that we have tended to relegate such matters to the category of things too difficult for us. To be honest, there are any number of projects in my life that I have measured from afar and bracketed as out-of-my-league, silly things like programming the VCR and running a marathon, and deep things like "love your enemies and pray for those who persecute you" (Matthew 5:43).

In the unconscious triage of life in which we sort our challenges into the doable, the conceivable and the incurable, most of us have put injustice in the last category. And understandably so. What in the world is more difficult? What is harder? Whether they are soldiers who murder the innocent, police who torture their prisoners or corrupt authorities who steal from the poor—violent and deceitful oppressors intimidate us.

Dissecting Injustice
Nothing is more intimidating than that which we do not understand. And it might be fair to acknowledge that the sin of injustice—the abuse of power—has not always been a well-developed theme of our devotional life. In the hundreds of sermons and Bible lessons we have heard (or preached), how many have dwelled on the sinful abuse of power? The problem is not that injustice has not been a *primary* theme of our devotional life; the problem is that it has rarely found a place even in our background knowledge of God's Word.

It would strike us as odd if we couldn't really explain what the Bible said about love, forgiveness, idolatry or adultery. If we could only vaguely say that God was generally in favor of the first two and opposed to the latter two, we might consider ourselves mere infants in Christ, feeding only on the milk and not the meat of the Word (1 Corinthians 3:1-2). Yet often our best summation of biblical teachings on justice might run something like this: "God's fair. The world's not. And it's all going to get sorted out in the end." As we might suspect, this is rather thin soup; it just doesn't equip us for dealing with the real world.

Imagine, for instance, that you and I are sitting together in an adult

Sunday-school class listening to a missionary, home on furlough, as she describes her work with street kids in Manila. We ask her to share what is most urgently on her heart, and she does. She is worried, she says, about three young girls whom she has been getting to know in her ministry. They are between the ages of twelve and fourteen, and they used to come around regularly for a hot meal and to hear Bible stories with the other street children. But she hasn't seen them for weeks. Tragically, when she asked around her ghetto neighborhood she learned that the girls had been abducted into a brothel and that they were being forced to serve as prostitutes. She wanted to talk to the police about it, but then she learned that it was the police who were actually running the brothel. Her heart is breaking for these girls, but she doesn't know what to do. She asks us, "Do you have any words of encouragement?"

Somehow in the face of her story it just doesn't seem adequate to say: "Heh. God's fair. The world's not. It will all get sorted out in the end." She just might reply, "Yes, but I love these girls. What am I supposed to do? These children are my neighbors; what would the Good Samaritan do?"

As our Sunday-school class tries to formulate a godly and loving response, what Scripture would immediately come to mind—verses that tell how God views this situation? What sermons would we recall—sermons about the promises God makes in his Word about such situations? What Bible-study lessons would spring to mind— teaching that would help us encourage our missionary about what should be done? How long could our Sunday-school class discuss this situation before running out of solid biblical material? Where I come from, most of us simply would express horror at the situation and recommend prayer. But we might struggle to articulate what we should pray for and what Scriptural truths we should base our prayers on.

Of course hundreds of Scriptural references apply to this missionary's situation. It's not that we are not devoted to God, or forgetful of the Bible, or uncaring. Rather, most of us simply don't have ready access to the biblical tools that God intends us to carry as his disciples into an unjust world.

But, praise God, this is a problem with a solution. It is possible to begin moving out of the paralysis of despair simply by coming to a better understanding of what lies in the darkness. If we ask God to give us an understanding of injustice, he will grant our prayer and transform us in the process. As the Scriptures promise,

> The LORD gives wisdom, and from his mouth come knowledge and understanding. He holds victory in store for the upright, he is a shield to those whose walk is blameless, for he guards the course of the just and protects the way of his faithful ones. Then you will understand what is right and just and fair—every good path. For wisdom will enter your heart, and knowledge will be pleasant to your soul. Discretion will protect you, and understanding will guard you. Wisdom will save you from the ways of wicked men, from men whose words are perverse, who leave the straight paths to walk in dark ways, who delight in doing wrong and rejoice in the perverseness of evil, whose paths are crooked and who are devious in their ways. (Proverbs 2:6-15)

Instead of confronting injustice from a blurry distance as something dark, vague and overwhelming, we can examine it, dissect it, lay bare its component parts and demystify its power. Therefore our initial inquiry is a simple diagnosis of the problem: Why is seeking justice so hard?

Two Stories of Injustice
Samson Gahungu is from Burundi, a small African country nestled between Rwanda, Tanzania and the Democratic Republic of the Congo (formerly Zaire). At the tender age of thirteen, he says, "I confessed my sins and obtained salvation." Eventually God's call on his life led him to become the leader of the Evangelical Quaker

church in Burundi. He became a teacher and administrator at a Quaker school in northern Burundi and is the proud father of nine children.

Samson's country is torn by the same ethnic conflict between Hutus and Tutsis that erupted into genocide in Rwanda. Samson is a Hutu, but he has worked for unity in his country as head of the peace and reconciliation department of the Burundi Council of Churches. In February of 1996, however, leaders of the Tutsi-dominated military regime sent soldiers to arrest Samson and hundreds of other prominent Hutu leaders throughout the country. Samson was transported to the capital city of Bujumbura and thrown in prison on charges of genocide, flowing from ethnic violence that occurred several years before. Without an opportunity to confront the charges against him or to defend himself, Samson languished in a horrifically overcrowded prison for more than a year and a half.

In a letter from prison Samson described his ordeal:

> To me, prison is stagnation; handcuffed in a cell; crouching in a tiny space, behind walls and bars where you can only see the sky; doing everything in one half-lit, unventilated room, a room enclosed on six sides—fortified walls, roof and floor smoke blackened and filth-stained; deprivation of family and friends; a stream of endless thoughts, monotony, worry, discouragement, loneliness, sickness, hunger, thirst and discomfort.[2]

Perhaps even more painful than these deprivations was Samson's heartache for his wife, who, sick with malaria, was left alone to care for their nine children.

> Recently she [Samson's wife] brought our last born (a three-year-old boy) to visit me. I was extremely happy to see him again, though he was terrified at seeing me in the inmates' uniform behind iron bars. My happiness was mixed with sorrow, because my wife is suffering with malaria. Further she left our children

wandering around because of prevailing uncertainty which maintains them in permanent displacement. Furthermore, they have lost all their belongings in those nomadic-like conditions. They have lost weight because they are homeless and the sadness resulting from our separation oppresses them too much.[3]

Though suffering these overwhelming trials, Samson wrote: "Even though my burden is too heavy, I know that my Lord loves me. I carry my cross imitating the way Jesus carried my sins at Calvary."[4]

Later there was a change in leadership of the military regime, and the International Justice Mission was able to make inquiry on his behalf. Finally the Burundi government dropped all charges against Samson and released him to his family.

But as the Jesus of Calvary well knows, Samson and his family suffered deeply under this abuse of power by authorities. Jesus knows all about it because he too was falsely arrested on trumped up charges and subjected to abuse. Looking at both of their stories, will help us dissect the dynamics of injustice.

The Two Components of Injustice: Coercion and Deception

Wherever we find the perpetration of injustice, we will find two components: coercion and deception. They may work separately or in combination. Scripture repeatedly affirms this principle.

His [the wicked man's] victims are *crushed,* they *collapse;* they fall *under his strength.* (Psalm 10:10)

The wicked *draw the sword* and *bend the bow* to bring down the poor and needy. (Psalm 37:14)

The mouth of the righteous is a fountain of life, but the mouth of the wicked *conceals violence.* (Proverbs 10:11 NRSV)

The scoundrel's methods are wicked, he makes up evil schemes

to destroy the poor *with lies,* even when the plea of the needy is
just. (Isaiah 32:7)

Quite naturally, most of us feel pretty uncomfortable with coercion
and deception. We don't know much about them and frankly we don't
want to. When was the last time we attended or led a Bible study about
coercion? When was the last time we heard or preached a sermon
series on the way powerful people use deception to hurt those who are
weak?

Yet any serious understanding of injustice requires a serious study
of these two rather unattractive topics. As a result, even though the
Bible repeatedly discusses injustice and oppression and calls us to be
engaged in a godly struggle against these sins, these subjects can feel
very foreign to our devotional life as Christians. So although we
suspect that injustice is a *major* topic for God, we are so ill-equipped
to confront it that we begin to believe that it could only be meant as a
minor topic for us.

Of course it need not be so. A little understanding can go a long
way toward dispelling the intimidating mystique of injustice, and
fortunately the Bible is full of teaching material. We can, for example,
return to the arrests of Samson Gahungu and Jesus and discover some
specifics about the first component of injustice: coercion.

Coercion Laid Bare

Coercion is the compelling or constraining of a person to act against
his or her free will—usually by physical force, the threat of force or
the threat of some other dire consequence. This is the ugly "or else!"
wielded by the oppressor. It can be as blatant as a blow to the head or
as subtle as a hint of economic destitution. But it is always some sort
of force that the oppressor wields to take from those who are in a
weaker position.

In Samson's case the coercive force was exercised by soldiers with guns who used the implicit threat of force to detain him and throw him in prison. Similarly, as Matthew describes it, Jesus was arrested by "a large crowd *armed* with swords and clubs, *sent* from the chief priests and the elders of the people" (Matthew 26:47). In this brief passage we see three important elements of coercion.

The first element: Weapons and brute force. Those who came to arrest Jesus approached with the traditional tools of coercive power: weapons of violence and superior numbers. Injustice is perpetrated by those who are able to force others to submit to their will, usually by hard physical force. And here is the point: As uncomfortable as it is to face, we need to know that when we see the words *injustice* or *oppression* in the Bible, God is talking about a most untidy sin. This sin has behind it, veiled or unveiled, the forces of physical violence—bullets that tear a body, blows that injure a brain, pressure that crushes a bone. When the soldiers came to arrest Samson and arrest Jesus, they came prepared to physically hurt them or anyone who would stop them. We need to acknowledge this unpleasant reality.

This seems obvious, and in many cases of the most brutal injustice, it is. On the other hand, a great deal of injustice is perpetrated with the realities of coercive force deeply in the background. At one time in the American South, African-American citizens may have seemed to lookers-on as if they were simply uninterested in voting or in sitting in the front of the bus. Nothing about it seemed overtly coercive; it was just "the way things are down here." What Rev. Martin Luther King Jr. and Rosa Parks did was expose the ugly violence that actually kept African-Americans from the polls or from front of the bus. To expose the coercion that was actually taking place, they did simple but courageous things: they kept trying to register to vote and trying to ride at the front of the bus until the authorities beat them with clubs or dragged them off to jail. These strategies proved very effective; they are a useful lesson for looking at much injustice that we might view as "just the way things are" in this world.

In India, for example, many people look at the fifteen million children sold into bonded labor and think, *That's just the way things are.* But as I learned from Shama, a ten-year-old girl in southern India, her slavery didn't just happen; it was imposed on her by coercion—a coercion more subtle than that which Samson faced but no less brutal.

Two years ago, when Shama's younger sister Mubarak was born, there were complications. Shama's impoverished family urgently needed twenty-five dollars for medical assistance. They didn't have the money, so they had to visit the local *mudalali,* or moneylender. He agreed to advance them the amount, but in exchange Shama's father had to sell her into servitude, manufacturing cigarettes for the mudalali.

Since she was eight years old Shama has been working off the debt. She sits in the same place on the floor closing the ends of cigarettes with a little knife from 7:00 a.m. to 8:00 p.m., taking only one fifteen-minute break for lunch. If she doesn't close enough cigarettes or shows up late, she is beaten. She works six days a week, and at the end of the week she gets her wages from the mudalali—about fifty cents. If she never spent any of her wages, it would take her a year to pay off her debt. Her family, however, desperately needs that fifty cents to survive each week. So after two years she is no closer to paying off the debt to the mudalali than when she started. If she is like most children who are sold into bonded labor, she will spend her entire childhood this way.

At a moment of medical crisis and economic desperation the mudalali used the coercive threat of economic destitution to compel Shama's parents to sell her into servitude. The mudalali's deal: sell Shama under his conditions, or else go without medical care. Once sold, she cannot bargain for wages and she cannot escape her servitude unless she pays back the loan *in a lump sum.* Of course, since the mudalali determines the wage, he simply never pays her enough to ever accumulate such a sum. Through the coercion of economic desperation, the deception of hidden interest charges and the threat of abuse if she does not comply, the mudalali is able to capture Shama's income stream in perpetuity, rob her of her childhood and destroy any hope of her ever breathing a breath of freedom in her youth.

Subtle as it may all be, the coercion behind Shama's oppression would be quickly exposed the minute she refused (like Rev. Martin Luther King Jr. or Rosa Parks) to do what was expected of her. She would be assaulted, and her destitute family would be cut off from access to the resources needed to survive. Hidden or not, the blunt fact behind injustice is brute force.

The second element: The powers behind the force. Returning to Jesus' and Samson's arrests, we can see that those who exercised the coercive force—the soldiers who made the arrests—were actually *sent* by other people. In Jesus' case the armed men were "*sent* from the chief priests and the elders of the people" (Matthew 26:47). Likewise the soldiers who wielded the actual force that arrested and detained Samson were *sent* by authorities higher up a military chain of command. Coercion is thus generally exercised through two very different sets of people: those who actually wield the tools of naked force (that is, soldiers, police officers, thugs) and those who tell them where and when to wield them. We almost always pay attention to the former, those who actually carry the gun or the club. But as we plainly know from Christ's own story, the real players are the equivalents of the "chief priests and the elders of the people." They *sent* the thugs, and without their direction the "large crowd armed with swords and clubs" would likely be a bored group of ne'er-do-wells and lackeys still lounging around the local watering hole waiting for something to do.

There are, of course, occasions when soldiers or police are abusive on their own initiative, but usually they are sent on their coercive errands by those who have command over them. Even when soldiers or police use their own initiative to abuse others, those in command have the power to take away their tools of coercion (guns, clubs, handcuffs).

The third element: A claim to lawful authority. Coercion's third element is the claim to legitimacy. The only thing that distinguishes the police officer that arrests and the kidnapper who seizes is some claim to lawfulness, proper authority or legitimacy. Therefore those who send the soldiers and police usually do so under some formalized claim of legitimacy or proper authority. The religious elders in Jesus' case felt the need to trump up some criminal charge against Jesus to legitimize his detention and execution.[5] Likewise the Burundi authorities had to assert some claim against Samson to legitimize his arrest, so they accused him of genocide. Of course, the most abusive governments claim the power to detain *without* charge or trial, as the South African government did when I lived there in the 1980s. Under such circumstances—when the government need not establish *any* legitimate reason for its coercive actions—distinguishing the government agents from common kidnappers becomes difficult.

In this brief discussion we can see the three elements of coercion that make seeking justice so difficult. First, injustice is difficult to confront because (hidden or in-your-face) it involves the use or threat of physical violence. Second, while the coercive force of injustice is exercised by one person, the actual causal agent behind the coercion is usually someone else—someone who sends the one who wields the force. And third, behind the one who commands the exercise of force is a claim to legitimacy or proper authority—a claim which, if not sustained, removes the distinction between lawful authority and common criminality. Some oppressors are willing to look like criminals in the eyes of their community, nation or the world, but most are not.

Deception Exposed

The other major component of injustice is deception. Sometimes injustice is perpetrated almost purely by deception—that is, when oppressors lie in order to rob victims. In India the mudalali lied to Shama about the rate of interest he is actually charging on her loan. In South Africa the wealthy white landowners would steal their poor black neighbor's plot of land by working in collusion with government officials to raise the land taxes beyond what the poor farmers could pay and then purchasing their neighbor's farm from the government for about one dollar. The prophet Micah described the same deception in Bible times: "They covet fields and seize them, and houses, and take them. They defraud a man of his home, a fellowman of his inheritance" (Micah 2:2). Isaiah too said that oppressors devise "evil schemes to destroy the poor with lies" (Isaiah 32:7).

More frequently, however, deception is used in combination with coercion. As Proverbs observes, "the mouth of the wicked conceals violence" (Proverbs 10:11 NRSV). This is a critical point. The reason that injustice is difficult to confront is that those who perpetrate it almost always lie about it. Most of us are not very comfortable entering into a world where we have to deal with people who do not tell the truth, but if we are going to enter the struggle for justice in the world, we must get used to the idea that we are entering a world where people lie—a lot.

Moreover—and this is critically important—if we are struggling against injustice we are dealing with people of power or authority who abuse that power and lie about it. We are not talking about your average lowdown drug dealer, repeat offender or ghetto crook. We are talking about the most exalted and esteemed people of power and authority in the society—these are the liars we are dealing with when we confront the deepest injustice. Therefore those of us who have been raised with a respect for authority and a Romans 13 deference to government officials must, if we are going to seek biblical justice, accustom ourselves to the unsettling reality that those who have power and authority are not only capable of abusing that power but are capable of going to great lengths to lie about it.

We are not called to gratuitous disrespect for those in authority, quite the contrary. We are to render to them their due, pray for them and submit to their authority as they exercise it in accordance with God's will. But at all times, rulers and authorities remain fallen creatures capable of great and dark sin. King David not only abused his authority to steal Uriah's wife, he also ended up murdering Uriah to cover it up. Nathan, however, had to expose the lie. The "princes" and "officials" of Jerusalem not only "killed people to make unjust gain," but they also used the prophets to "whitewash these deeds" (Ezekiel 22). Accordingly, Ezekiel had to expose the lie. Imagine the context Micah faced among the respected authorities and rulers of Israel: "Both hands are skilled in doing evil; *the ruler* demands gifts, *the judge* accepts bribes, *the powerful* dictate what they desire— they all conspire together" (Micah 7:3). But God called Micah to expose the lies. "But as for me," declared Micah, "I am filled with power, with the spirit of the LORD, and with justice and might, to declare to Jacob his transgression, to Israel his sin" (Micah 3:8).

The obvious need for us to confront deceitful rulers and to challenge unlawful authorities may make us uneasy, but Jesus has never left any wiggle room for divided loyalties. As Peter said, "We must obey God rather than men!" (Acts 5:29) When we hear God's call to enter the struggle for justice, we must remember the profound biblical truth: "Everyone who does evil hates the light, and will not come into the light for fear that his deeds will be exposed" (John 3:20).

Deception in the Philippines

I began to learn some of the hard truths about deception in the Philippines in 1989. I was sent to the Philippines by the Lawyers Committee for Human Rights to try to figure out why the new government, which had taken over from the corrupt dictator Ferdinand

Marcos, had not brought any successful prosecutions against the police or military for ongoing human-rights abuses. Cory Aquino was president, having recently come to power in a bloodless "people power" revolution that followed after her husband, the nation's leading political dissident, was murdered by Marcos' cronies. When Cory Aquino took over the presidency, she inherited two things from Marcos: an abusive police and military, and a dirty war against a Marxist guerrilla movement in the countryside. President Aquino came to power as a human-rights activist—having seen her own husband murdered by an oppressive dictator—but she didn't seem capable of stopping her own army from killing, raping and torturing innocent people as they went about their struggle against the communist insurgency.

When I went over to live in the Philippines to find out why this was so, I thought I would start with the most obvious case: the Lupao massacre. Anyone who read the newspapers in the Philippines had heard of the Lupao massacre. Like a smaller version of the American Mai Lai massacre, soldiers from the 14th infantry battalion of the Philippine Army murdered seventeen unarmed villagers (including six children and two elderly) and wounded eight more. A small handful of guerillas had spent the previous night in the village. In the early morning as an army patrol approached the small cluster of huts, the guerillas managed to shoot and kill the leader of the army patrol. By the time army reinforcements arrived, the guerillas were long gone, up the mountains. Out of frustration the army soldiers herded the villagers out of the rice paddies where they had been hiding and began to mow them down with gunfire.

After the incident, the army reported that they had "managed to kill 11 NPAs [New People's Army guerillas] on the spot,"[6] had captured five and had taken two additional wounded NPA members to a hospital. All of this, of course, turned out to be false—for none of the victims were guerillas. They were well-known peasants from the village, their grandparents and children. Later the army claimed that the civilians had been killed in the crossfire during the firefight with the guerillas and added that some of the civilians had been killed when the guerillas destroyed their houses with grenades. But all seven survivors of the massacre told a different story, and the close-range gunshot wounds of the civilian victims proved that the army's second claim was false. As the army's own provost marshal concluded, the villagers "were deliberately killed by the soldiers of the 14th IB,"[7] who were trying to "cover up" the murders. It took some time, but finally the soldiers of that battalion were brought before a court-martial to face charges for the massacre.

To everyone's surprise, however, the court-martial acquitted all the accused soldiers. According to President Aquino, the acquittal resulted from the "noncooperation of certain witnesses."[8] According to the presiding officer of the court-marshal, "Twenty witnesses failed to testify which resulted in insufficiency of evidence."[9] The military prosecutors said that they "got little support from the victims, some of whom refused to testify."[10]

This was enormously puzzling to me. On the one hand, I could understand why the victims might not have shown up to testify. First of all, the trial was not held in their province, but inside the army military headquarters in Manila. Testifying at the trial would require a nine-hour roundtrip journey for each day of the trial. More important, when you have seen with your own eyes, as they had, that the army is capable of murdering innocent civilians, it is rather intimidating to walk into *their* headquarters and accuse them face to face. Who knows what will happen to you on your way there or on your way back.

Nevertheless, I also knew that people who had seen their own family members murdered were generally passionate enough about the injustice to do just about anything to see the truth be told. No one in the military could give me very satisfying reasons why the surviving victims of the massacre would not show up, so I decided to go out to Lupao and ask them myself.

Uncovering the Survivors' Truth

I traveled the way the survivors would have come. I took a rusted, noisy bus out of the urban sprawl of Manila and headed into the countryside of Tarlac and Neuva Ecija. There is nothing quite as green as the rice paddies that carpet these rural provinces, and it's always so refreshing to get out of the choking smog of Manila. My bus dropped me off in a busy market in San Jose, where I hitched a ride into the village of Lupao. I walked over to the dilapidated municipal hall and asked if anyone knew where attorney Edward Limos lived. They all did, of course, since Ed was just about the only lawyer in the area. The village police corporal gave me a ride on the back of his motorcycle to the lawyer's house. Ed was a shy young man with a soft face and a gentle smile. He was obviously very smart, and amid all the meekness one could clearly see the etched lines of resolution that ran from his eyes to his broad cheek bones. Attorney Limos lived and worked in Manila, but he had grown up in Lupao and had taken a personal interest in supporting the survivors of the Lupao massacre in their search for justice.

Ed introduced me to the mustached mayor of Lupao, and together we took a ride in the village ambulance out to the tiny hamlet of Namulandayan where the massacre had actually taken place. The cluster of huts sat at the feet of sharp green mountains, and I could readily see how the guerillas could make such a quick retreat into the highland mist. I saw the charred remains of the victims' bamboo huts lying flat in the red mud, and Ed showed me where the villagers had been rounded up and shot in the rice paddy.

I talked with several of the survivors. As usual, it was all rather businesslike until I really let my eyes meet theirs. Especially Merissa's—a beautiful eight-year-old girl whose hand had been shot off by the soldiers' high-powered weapons. As old as the story was to Ed,

I could tell that he just couldn't stand thinking about what Merissa had been through.

So I asked them, "Why didn't you go to the court-martial and testify against the soldiers who did this?"

"Oh, but we did!" they said. I looked at them puzzled.

"Oh yes," Ed said. "All seven of the survivors testified at the court-martial, and they positively identified at least four of the defendant soldiers."

I showed them the quote of the presiding officer of the court-martial claiming that "twenty witnesses failed to testify," and the statement by the military defense attorney that "the survivors had failed to identify any soldiers involved in the alleged massacre."

Ed, who had accompanied all the survivors to the trial, was stunned by these statements. "We had seven witnesses, and they all showed up. None of the prosecution's witnesses failed to appear."

The Evidence Tells the Story

There was the proof. Ed handed me the transcript of the court-martial, and sure enough, the testimony of all the survivors was recorded in black and white, along with the names of the four defendant soldiers whom they had positively identified. In fact, the survivors described to me what they had to go through to attend the trial. They woke up at 3:00 a.m. each day to perform their farm chores before leaving for Manila by five o'clock so they could be at the army camp by 9:30 a.m. Unable to afford overnight accommodations in Manila, they had to return each night to Lupao—arriving at around 11:00 at night. In fact, the trial had to be postponed for a time so that Ed could raise some more money to pay for the victims' transportation costs.

One of the survivors, Conchita Carnate, had seen her own husband, Ernesto, bayoneted to death while pleading with the soldiers in the middle of the Lupao rice paddy. She had gone to the court-martial, had broken down under the intimidating presence of all the soldiers, but had gone on to point out her husband's murderer. I showed her President Aquino's statement that the verdict acquitting all the soldiers "was no whitewash since there was no substantial evidence to convict the accused due to the noncooperation of certain witnesses." Mrs. Carnate responded: "We went there to the hearings. We were able to identify the killers. They should be in jail."

I read the entire transcript of the trial many times. There was nothing lacking in the testimony or other evidence against the accused. This is what happened. Initially, the accused soldiers testified that the civilians had been accidentally killed in the crossfire between the guerillas and the army. Then, after the testimony of the survivors and the physical evidence made it clear that this could not be true, they changed their story. Two of the soldiers who had been specifically identified by the survivors took the stand and admitted that their original testimony was false. They admitted that the civilians in Lupao had been deliberately killed by the soldiers. But in a brand-new twist they claimed that the four soldiers who had actually done the killing were not part of their unit, and therefore were not among the defendants before the court. These four soldiers, they said, had been transferred to duty in a remote province.

This patently self-serving testimony was never cross-examined. The four mystery soldiers were never located. And the court-martial heard no further evidence. They simply acquitted the accused and told the public and their president that the surviving witnesses never showed up to make their case.

How Deception Conceals Coercion

In this painful story we can learn a lot about the deception that makes the search for justice so difficult. Obviously, it is deception that conceals violence. Out of frustration and anger, these soldiers and their commanders abused their authority and power to take the lives of seventeen innocent and vulnerable villagers. To cover up the injustice, massive deception was applied to the coercive force. To see this, it might be helpful to look at the dynamics of coercion reviewed earlier as they apply to this case.

First, the soldiers stole the lives of these victims through the blunt brutality of bayonets and gunfire. Second, the soldiers are part of a chain of command. They were *sent* by others under orders to secure the vicinity. Those who sent them were responsible for equipping them with their bayonets and guns and for supervising how they used them. Third, the soldiers used their bayonets and guns under a claim of lawful authority and legitimacy. Ostensibly, they were protecting the population from the terrorism of the Marxist guerillas and protecting the legitimate government of the people of the Philippines.

All the lies that subsequently flowed out of these events were aimed at obscuring the truth about the nature of the coercion involved. With almost every act of injustice there is a natural checklist of lies that tracks the three points above. The oppressor will try to deceive others about three issues:

☐ the use of coercive force—that is, who was hurt, what force was used and who used it

☐ who was responsible for *sending* those who used the coercive force

☐ whether the use of force was legitimate or lawful

First, the soldiers deceived people; they lied about *who was hurt,* claiming that it was guerilla soldiers who had been killed. Then, conceding that civilians had been killed, they tried to lie about *who had killed* the civilians, claiming first that the guerillas had killed them with grenades. Later, admitting that the army soldiers had killed civilians, they claimed that these deaths were not unlawful because they were inadvertent consequences of a legitimate firefight with terrorists. When this proved false, they returned to the *who killed* question and claimed that soldiers from another unit had actually done the killing. In the midst of all of this the army never called to account the commanding officers who had sent the soldiers to Lupao, the

commanders who equipped them and trained them and the commanders who supervised them at the scene. The whole matter was dismissed
as the work of four rogue soldiers from another unit who could never
be located and for whom no one could take responsibility.

In every case of injustice the nature of the deception is going to be
different, but in almost every case the oppressor is going to try very
hard to hide the true nature of the coercion under which the victims
have been abused. The oppressor will try to lie about at least one of
the following questions:

☐ *What coercion, if any, was applied?* In Shama's case, the moneylender denies that there is a coercive contract for bonded labor and
claims that the child is "only an apprentice learning a skill," or "a free
laborer working for wages."

☐ *Who, if any one, was hurt?* The brothel owner in Cambodia lies
about the child's age and claims that she works as a prostitute by her
own free will and is doing what she wants.

☐ *Who applied the coercion?* The Philippine Army claims it was the
guerillas who killed the villagers.

☐ *Who sent or exercised authority over the one who applied the
coercion?* The Rio de Janeiro police deny any connection to the
death-squad that is murdering unwanted street children.

☐ *Was the application of coercion lawful or legitimate?* The Burundi
military claims legitimacy for Mr. Gahungu's detention because he is
a criminal who has committed acts of genocide.

In each of these cases the deceptions were exposed, but the lies
made it very difficult to seek justice for the victims. Many times even
the most senior authorities who exercise power in these situations are
unable to vindicate the rights of the victims because they themselves
are deceived about the nature of the coercion. I do not believe, for
example, that President Aquino was *unwilling* to seek justice for the
victims of the Lupao massacre; rather, she was herself a victim of the
lies of her subordinates and thus *unable* to render justice. One might

argue that she accepted her subordinates' representations too uncritically, but this is a different point than arguing that she was a coconspirator in the crimes. Again, when we discuss intervention strategies in the next chapters, it will be helpful to remember that injustice can be perpetrated through the ignorance (albeit, often willful ignorance) as well as through the intentional abuses of senior officials and authorities.

Coercion and Deception: Oppressors' Tools to Prevent Rescue

Oppressors use coercion and deception as tools not only to carry out injustice but also to keep rescuers from coming to the aid of the victim. Remember that injustice is the abuse of power by the strong over the weak. If victims had as much power as oppressors, they wouldn't be vulnerable and wouldn't be abused. If Shama wasn't so poor, she couldn't be taken advantage of. If the street girls weren't physically weaker, they couldn't be abducted into prostitution.

Protecting those who are vulnerable usually means bringing a countervailing power to bear on their behalf. When World Vision provides Shama's family with a low-interest loan and skill training, she and her family have economic power to resist the mudalali's coercion. When the International Justice Mission leads a detachment of Bombay police into a brothel where a young girl is being held in forced prostitution, she has a countervailing force on her side that allows her to walk away from the pimp's coercion. When the military police arrest and incarcerate soldiers who would shoot unarmed villagers, those villagers have a countervailing force on their side that protects them from the abusive soldiers' coercion.

What oppressors must do, therefore, is isolate their victims from those who might come to their aid. As we discussed before, no oppressors are powerful enough to overcome all the forces of truth and justice that humanity could amass against them. So they must keep their victims isolated from those who might bring a countervailing power to bear on the victims' behalf. To do so, they will use their two favorite tools: coercion and deception.

If possible, oppressors will simply use deception. First, if they can, they will make it look like nothing is wrong—like no one's being hurt. Or they will make it hard to figure out who is committing the abuse. Or they will make it seem like the victims deserve the abuse or brought it on themselves. These will all be obfuscation and deceptions designed to keep anyone from coming to the victims' aid.

If necessary, oppressors will use the *threat* of coercion to keep their victims isolated. At a minimum they will try to create an atmosphere of intimidation so that everyone is afraid even to ask the questions that will allow others to learn the truth about the victims' plight. Because they are relying on deception, oppressors cannot tolerate open inquiry. If there is one thing they hate, it's questions. People may openly suspect them of abuse and oppression, but if everyone is too intimidated to *prove* it, the oppressors will succeed.

Finally, if people get too close to the truth or to the victim, oppressors may actually use coercion to physically stop the intervention. I've had soldiers point their guns at me outside a military detention center and make it clear that they were prepared to shoot me if I kept bugging them about two prisoners who were being held incommunicado within their camp. Sometimes oppressors are indeed prepared to kill, as evidenced by the scores of lawyers and journalists who are murdered every year trying to expose the truth about injustice in the harsher places around the world. Often, however, oppressors simply want to scare people away. They wouldn't seriously hurt them and often they simply couldn't, but if they can deceive people about their coercive power, that is often as good as actually having the power. For them the result is the same. Their victims are alone, unprotected, utterly vulnerable. The victims can only cry out in isolation: "Why, O Lord, do you stand far off? Why do you hide yourself in times of trouble?"

God may be asking similar questions—not of himself but of his people: "And the LORD looked and was displeased that there was no justice. He saw that there was no one, he was appalled that there was no one to intervene." "Then I heard the voice of the Lord saying, "Whom shall I send? And who will go for us?" (Isaiah 6:8; 59:15-16).

Incidents of injustice are not just something that happen in an unfair world. God is appalled by them and calls us to seek justice. Oppressors can be intimidating, but in studying how they work—through coercion and deception—we can prepare ourselves to stand up to them. We *can* do something. The next two chapters offer some specifics about how to investigate the deceptions and how to intervene on behalf of the victims.

Ten

Investigating
the Deceptions

LET'S RETURN BRIEFLY TO THE MISSIONARY MENTIONED IN the previous chapter, the one who came to visit us in our adult Sunday-school class and who was heartbroken over the young girls abducted into a brothel operated by corrupt police in her neighborhood. It doesn't really matter to our story where the brothel is because it could be just about anywhere—Manila, Bombay, Lagos, Rio de Janeiro, Kiev, New Orleans. Regardless of the specific context, the same predictable rules of injustice apply. As we have seen, these girls are victims of coercion and deception. The burning question in the heart of the missionary is, Can anyone do anything about it?

Our Spiritual but Practical Calling

To provide an answer for her and the many others facing injustice firsthand, we will have to get very practical. To some Christians the discussion of the actual ways and means of fighting injustice might seem, well, *too* practical. It all might sound rather unspiritual, all-too-human, even unholy. In their discomfort some will want to say, "Our struggle is not against flesh and blood, but against the rulers, against the authorities, against the powers of this dark world and against the spiritual forces of evil in the heavenly realms" (Ephesians 6:12). But Jesus, who was not too spiritual for this world two thousand years ago and still isn't today, knew that the "powers of this dark world" and "the spiritual forces of evil in the heavenly places" are manifested here and now in very real sin, suffering and hurt. And he counteracted those forces with acts of love. Christ has called us to do the same.

Christians of mature faith know that love is both a deeply mystical and a profoundly practical calling. In some mysterious way, when we feed the hungry, visit the sick and clothe the naked, we do it for him also (Matthew 25). Jesus' model for love, a nameless Samaritan, messed up his clothes and his schedule by picking up a stranger who lay wounded and beaten in a ditch (Luke 10). Acts of love like this are so important to God that when the Israelites couldn't be bothered with the workaday practicalities of what it takes "to loose the chains of injustice" and "to set the oppressed free," God stopped listening to their prayers (Isaiah 58:1-6).

It's worth remembering that an entire book of the Bible is all about a woman's very practical efforts to stop the violent deceptions of an abusive government official—the book of Esther. Christians looking for "spirituality" will want to skip it because God isn't mentioned in the entire book. But anyone who reads it will see why God included it in his divine revelation to humanity. God was not too spiritual to work through the courageous faithfulness of one woman to stop the wholesale slaughter of the Jewish people at the hands of an evil Persian prime minister.

Whatever action God has called his people to do, the giants of the faith have always understood that it is worth doing with real-world excellence. They know that their abilities or gifts depend on the empowering of the Holy Spirit, but whatever they bring to the work in the way of study, of knowledge, of technical expertise, they "work at it with all their heart, as working for the Lord" (Colossians 3:23). God is not interested in crosscultural missionaries who are too spiritual to bother preaching in a language that the people can actually understand. He is not interested in missionary doctors too spiritual to bother operating on the organ that is actually diseased. He is not interested in relief workers too spiritual to bother airlifting the food supplies to the country that actually has the famine. He is interested in people who give their all to the tasks before them.

As God calls us to seek justice, he bids us to equip ourselves with some basic knowledge of what it takes to pursue the call with excellence. He does not presume that we are ready but beckons us, "*Learn to do right!* Seek justice, encourage the oppressed. Defend the cause of the fatherless, plead the case of the widow" (Isaiah 1:17). Loving those girls abducted into prostitution by abusive authorities is a very practical, deeply spiritual affair, and something worth learning a thing or two about.

As we saw from the previous chapter, rescuing these girls, or any victims of injustice, means overcoming the deception and coercion of the oppressor. Since these are two very different tasks, it's worth looking at them separately. In this chapter we learn how to tackle the first task, that of exposing deception. Chapter eleven tells us how to accomplish the second task—intervening for the victims.

Exposing deception can be described as a process of three steps, and these steps greatly overlap: gathering the facts, substantiating the facts by asking the appropriate questions and collecting all the evidence.

The First Step: Get the Facts

To uncover an oppressor's deception we must bring the facts of injustice into the light of day. We need to learn the truth about the coercion of the oppressor (the victim, the injury, the method and the perpetrator), the sponsor of the oppressor (the one who sends or commands the oppressor) and the oppressor's claim to legitimacy (the lawfulness or proper authority behind the coercion).

Factual investigation is generally difficult, however, because we have several obstacles to confront: the victims themselves, the need for special expertise and the risk of danger when we challenge oppressors' lies.

The first obstacle: The victims themselves and their advocates. This first obstacle may seem strange, but it's true. Most victims of injustice and their loving advocates, at some level, expect justice without having to supply all the facts. And that's understandable. In fact, there are several reasons why they don't naturally offer investigators the facts of the injustice.

1. Victims feel no need to note the facts since they have no doubts about what happened—after all, they were there. To victims, the facts are not in question. Consequently, even though many of the facts may be known, they are not noted as part of the story and do not come to light. Generally, people feel so passionately about the larger abuse they have suffered or seen others suffer that they simply do not focus on the particulars of the situation—things that seem relatively trivial in the larger tragedy of the story.

If a girl has been abducted into a brothel, for instance, she will probably not think that it matters very much what day of week it occurred. The same is true of a prisoner tortured by a group of police; his first description of the ordeal is unlikely to provide any information about which one of the individual police officers in the group actually struck him in the mouth with his baton. Unless specifically asked, he may dismiss the information as a wholly inconsequential detail—especially compared with the pain of such a blow. Similarly, if we simply ask an impoverished widow to tell us about the time the gang of armed men sent by the owner of the hacienda destroyed her little house and pushed her off her land, we have a 50 percent chance that she will tell us the whole story—for hours perhaps—without ever telling us the date it occurred. If we don't think to specifically ask, we will walk away with a tragic story but one that never happened in a specific point in time. More broadly, therefore, if we are not very intentional about our investigation, we will miss many pertinent facts.

2. The victim's sympathetic advocates generally feel uncomfortable asking the "how do you know" questions. Ferreting out the facts of the abuse from the victims or their advocates requires that one always ask an awkward question, "How do you know what you know?"

Imagine again our missionary in our Sunday-school class who tells us about "the girls who have been abducted into the brothel." It is quite unnatural for most people to ask the missionary, "Well, how do you know that these girls have actually been abducted into a brothel?" Your missionary has told you something painful from her heart and you want to express sympathy—which you can't possibly begin to express if you don't communicate that you believe her. And you can't very well express that you believe her if you ask a question that indicates doubt about what she said. Fundamentally, gentle and sympathetic people do not naturally engage in cross-examination of someone who has revealed pain and suffering from their heart. Thus they never ask the questions and never get the answers that are necessary for actually determining the facts of the abuse.

3. Victims and their advocates easily forget that their story is going to have to be proved to people who don't want to believe it and in the face of vigorous, lying denials from their oppressors. If we begin with the facts of the abuse as they are relayed through the narration of the victims and their closest friends and supporters, we actually end up with very few of the facts that we need in order to seek justice. So to get the necessary facts, we need to conduct a very intentional investigation, reminding the victims and their advocates of the need for proof—the specific details of the situation, trivial though they may seem. In the end these details will lead to a much stronger case against their oppressors and a greater possibility that they will be brought to account.

4. There are some facts that the poorest and most vulnerable people in the world simply don't know—like how to spell their own name. Many poor and underprivileged people don't have the luxury of keeping track of facts. Most of the Rwandan massacre survivors that I interviewed didn't own a watch, so they couldn't tell me what time of day or night the worst event of their life occurred. Child prostitution may be illegal, but if the girl doesn't know her own age we don't know if she is legally a child or not. If the bonded laborer can't read or write or do simple arithmetic, then she will never think to obtain a written record of her indebtedness and she will have no idea what rate of interest she is being charged—although it may be more than 1,000 percent a year.

The second obstacle: The need for specialized knowledge and skill. Getting the facts is also difficult because it often requires some sort of special expertise. Without the help of legal, medical and criminal-investigation experts, some investigations would not be possible.

Legal experts. As a preliminary matter it's important to receive help in figuring out what facts we need in order to prove that the abuse took place. We may have to prove more than we think. Lawyers call this *proving the elements of the crime.* For instance, the crime of rape generally consists of two elements: (1) sexual contact to which the other person (2) did not consent. In different countries there will be different rules about what kind of sexual contact has to be proved, and different rules about what facts establish the absence of consent. Some countries, for instance, require that a girl or woman demonstrate that she actively resisted the alleged assailant. Other countries, however, recognize that a woman might feel too intimidated to resist actively or might think that by doing so she would risk further injury. Imagine a girl being attacked by a man with a gun and then being asked later to prove that she physically resisted her attacker. The absurdity of this has led to the abandonment of such requirements in most Western countries. However, in other parts of the world, especially in those countries with strong cultural biases against the rights of women, the law can be different. So we must know what facts need to investigated.

Occasionally, fewer facts are required than we might think. In India, for instance, many people concerned about bonded labor are discouraged by the difficulty of proving the bonded servitude when there is no contract or receipt to evidence the abusive relationship. Under Indian law, however, this evidentiary problem is supposed to be the moneylender's and not the laborer's. According to the law, the bonded laborer need only make a *claim* of bonded servitude, and then the law shifts the burden of proof to the mudalali to prove that the laborer is *not* in bonded servitude. Proving a negative is very hard to do—especially if you don't have a piece of paper. So now the absence of the contract is the mudalai's problem, not the bonded laborer's. At times some technical knowledge of the law not only frames the question that needs to be asked but also lightens the investigative load.

Medical experts. Sometimes, establishing the fact of the abuse and even the identity of the victim is a challenge. I can remember going out to participate in the exhumation of the body of a woman in the Philippines who had been brutally raped, tortured and murdered by a group of drunken army soldiers on the island of Eastern Samar. An eyewitness to the horror, the victim's brother, had escaped to tell the whole story. But we really needed the body of the victim to prove that the murder actually took place. So the brother lead us out to the site where he knew the soldiers had buried her body. But it wasn't there. Apparently, the soldiers had removed it. What were we to do now? How were we going to seek justice for this girl and her family if we couldn't even prove that something bad had happened to her? Fortunately, we had some forensic doctors with us, and they were able to sift through the soil and find more than sufficient tissue samples and other physical evidence to prove the brother's story.

Criminal investigation experts. Consider the three girls abducted into the brothel. How is the missionary going to establish the facts of such a story? *We* may believe what the missionary says, but if she can't explain in detail to skeptics who the girls are, where they are being held, why she thinks they are being "held" there, and—most importantly—*how* she knows each of these things, then she can't seek justice for them. Moreover, finding out all this information can be rather tricky. And I don't know many missionaries who have received relevant training for conducting such an investigation. That doesn't mean, however, that it can't be done. The International Justice Mission, for instance, has developed and deployed undercover techniques for locating such brothels, going inside and videotaping the girls that are being held there. But this is hard to do. At the International Justice Mission this is the work of highly experienced criminal investigators on our staff.

The third obstacle: The risk of physical harm. In getting the facts necessary to overcome deception, we meet with a third obstacle: the risk of physical danger. Many countries with the most brutal injustices are difficult to access, or they manifest a high level of civil unrest or random violence. Even in relatively accessible and stable environments, however, we may not feel safe asking a lot of questions around people who are violent, deceitful oppressors. We can, however, assess and manage the risks.

Not everyone shares the same vulnerabilities. What may be very dangerous for one person may be perfectly safe for another. For the victim of police torture to return to the police station and try to identify the name of the officer who committed the abuse would be very dangerous. But it may be perfectly safe for another person, armed with a description of the officer and a plausible pretext for being there, to find out the same basic information.

In most cases, we can determine who is at risk and why; then we can devise a strategy that reduces that risk to an acceptable level. It may be important, for instance, to provide some level of protection for witnesses. In the case involving the woman who had been raped and murdered by the drunken soldiers, we needed to provide protection for the brother who had survived the ordeal. A group of us escorted him to the local prosecutor's office to file the necessary papers, then we drove him and his family to another province where he could be maintained in a safe house until the next step in the proceedings.

There will always be contexts in which it is humanly impossible to operate safely, and in such circumstances there may indeed be nothing we can do. But at least we will be able to distinguish those situations from contexts that simply *feel* unsafe or are unsafe for a particular individual.

The Second Step: Substantiate the Facts by Asking the Right Questions

To overcome an oppressor's deception we must conduct a very intentional and systematic investigation of the facts. This includes making a comprehensive list of questions to be answered. As we have mentioned, the relevant questions will generally include the following:

☐ Who is the victim?

☐ What is the nature of the injury—how has the victim been hurt? Is the abuse or oppression continuing?

☐ What is the means or method of abuse or injury—how, when and where does the oppressor carry out this injury or abuse?

☐ Who is the perpetrator, and why does he or she commit the abuse?

☐ Is the person who actually performs the abuse sent by someone else or under a chain of command or authority? If so, who is the oppressor's commander or sponsor?

☐ Does the oppressor, the commander or sponsor claim some kind of legitimacy or lawful authority for the abuse? What is the basis for such a claim? Are the oppressor's actions legal in the society?

Generally, these are the questions that need answers. And as we seek answers, we must constantly ask, "How do we know what we think we know?" Every step of the way, this is the most urgent question. It's the most important question but the one most people forget to think hard about. How do we *know* the girls were abducted into a brothel? How do we *know* that the armed gang was sent by the landlord? Many times the answer sounds something like this: "Well, my brother said his neighbor heard about it from his coworker." Or, "Everybody knows it." Or, "His mother said she read about it in the newspaper." If so, then we have our work cut out for us.

This question is so important because, generally, when we take the information that we have and seek intervention on behalf of the victim, we are going to present the information to people who are not going to want to believe us—and the perpetrators are going to lie through their teeth to deny everything that we say. They are going to make up an alternate explanation for events. They are going to get their friends to lie in order to back them up. On the basis that the best defense is a good offense, oppressors will even assert some shameful, humiliating, dangerous allegations against us. In such a context it's mighty healthy to have thought a little bit about how we know what we think we know.

The Third Step: Collect All the Related Evidence
In a general sense we can know what we know (1) because of what the perpetrator admits, (2) because of what we or others have seen or heard firsthand and (3) because of what physical things indicate.

Information usually comes in three forms: What people have written down or recorded, called *documentary evidence.* What people say, called *testimonial evidence.* And what is indicated by material things (a scar, a footprint, a bullet hole), called *physical* or *demonstrative evidence.*

Documentary evidence. Usually the most powerful evidence, and the hardest to come by, comes from the words or conduct of the oppressors themselves. While conducting an investigation of bonded child labor, for instance, the International Justice Mission was able to capture on videotape a mudalali bragging about the hundreds of children he held in bonded servitude. How do we know these children are held in bonded servitude? Answer: The mudalali said so. Occasionally we can ask officials very pointed, specific questions about a person or a situation and force them to choose between admitting some piece of information or risk being caught publicly later on in a bald-faced lie. Occasionally we can get copies of an oppressor's own records that might prove a fact—like a military log book that records that a certain prisoner came into the camp at a certain time but hasn't been seen since. Sometimes oppressors will say something careless in public that will be recorded by a newspaper or camera.

Testimonial evidence. Most evidence, however, comes in the form of testimonial evidence or statements from witnesses—either from the victims or from other observers or participants. For example, if we can get the girls out of the brothel, they can tell us how they got there and who put them there. If the missing prisoner was seized from his home, his family members can tell us who came and got him, when and how, what they said and what they looked like. If sources can be developed within the paramilitary group, they can tell us who gives them their guns and pays for the gas in the truck.

Physical evidence. After we get the story, the asserted facts will either be supported or contradicted by "things"—the physical evidence. If the prisoner's wounds match his testimony, then we *know* he was tortured, not just because he says so but because the medical examination of his body also says so. If the spent shell casings match the ammunition that is distributed to the government army, then the physical evidence *corroborates* the villagers' story that the men who attacked the ethnic minority village were actually members of the military, in spite of their civilian clothes.

Thus by various investigative strategies it's possible to establish the facts of the victim's abuse and overcome the oppressor's deception. The missionary's story about the girls abducted into a brothel by police sounds hopeless at first. But if I tell you that we are able to obtain a surreptitious video of the girls in the brothel being offered for sex by men who can be identified as members of the local police, bringing about justice doesn't seem so hopeless anymore. Maybe we can take this information somewhere and get the girls released.

This is the power of factual information. It's usually hard to get, often *very* hard to get. But once we have isolated the needed information, we can devise a focused plan and mobilize the expertise and resources that are required to obtain it. Then we can go on to the next task—intervening on behalf of the victims.

Eleven

Intervening
for the Victims

OUR SECOND TASK IN SEEKING JUSTICE FOR THE OPPRESSED is to intervene on their behalf—to take the information to people or institutions that can help. As we have discussed, injustice is the abuse of power. Persons of power or authority use their power to take from those who are weak. To do so, the oppressor isolates the weaker individuals from those who might be able to bring counteracting power to bear on the victim's behalf. "I looked and saw all the oppression that was taking place under the sun: I saw the tears of the oppressed—and they have no comforter; power was on the side of their oppressors" (Ecclesiastes 4:1). Intervention, therefore, is the process by which the isolation of the weaker individual is overcome and power is introduced on the side of the weaker brother or sister. The term *intervene* literally means "to come in between." So when we intervene, we use the factual information that we have gathered to place a counteracting, protective power between the abuser and the victim. So it is that God is able to "rescue the poor from those too strong for them" (Psalm 35:10).

Effective intervention depends on the analysis of the appropriate *type* of intervention needed, the best *method* of intervention and the best *agent* of intervention. A proper analysis can help an advocate arrive at the intervention strategy that will have the greatest likelihood of bringing meaningful help to the victim. Of course, this analysis requires information, another reason why the comprehensive gathering of the facts about the abuse, the victim and the perpetrator is so important.

The First Step: Select the Appropriate Type of Intervention

The first step is to decide what *type* of intervention we will use. These categories overlap somewhat, but generally we have four broad options, with one or more being appropriate in any given case. The best choice is based largely on the victim's needs.

Victim rescue. "Defend the cause of the weak and fatherless; maintain the rights of the poor and oppressed. Rescue the weak and the needy; deliver them from the hand of the wicked" (Psalm 82:3-4).

This intervention is for the victim who is presently suffering abuse—the prisoner being illegally detained or tortured, the girl being held in prostitution, the child in bonded servitude. The victim needs to be delivered or rescued from the ongoing oppression. Samson Gahungu needs to be released from his prison cell. Shama needs to be set free from her obligation to the mudalali. The girls in the Bombay brothel need to be rescued from the coercive forces that hold them in the brothel.

Perpetrator accountability. "In arrogance the wicked man hunts down the weak, who are caught in the schemes he devises. . . . Break the arm of the wicked and evil man; call him to account for his wickedness that would not be found out" (Psalm 10:2, 15).

Perpetrator accountability is the appropriate intervention after the abuse has taken place. The injury can't be undone, but the perpetrators can be brought to account for their abuse, and compensation or restoration sought for the victim. Shama's mudalali needs to be arrested and fined or imprisoned for the fraud, assault and oppression perpetrated against

Shama. Rosa's alleged assailant needs to be arrested and forced to face the charges against him. The police operating the brothel need to be identified, dismissed from the police force and punished for their kidnapping and sexual assault. The soldiers responsible for the Lupao massacre need to be brought to account for their murders.

Structural prevention. "[Defend] the fatherless and the oppressed, in order that man, who is of the earth, may terrify no more" (Psalm 10:18).

This intervention is necessary to ensure that the victim and other vulnerable individuals and groups are not abused again. Perpetrator accountability is often the most important ingredient for structural prevention, for it stops the bad guys from continuing the abuse and it creates powerful disincentives for others who might be likewise tempted to abuse their power. In fact, without perpetrator accountability, it's almost impossible to keep the abuse from occurring again. This is why it is so important to not only set Shama free, but to have her mudalali arrested. Moreover, he probably needs to be sanctioned with something more severe than a fine, or else, because of the extremely high profitability of bonded servitude, he may be willing to carry on and simply factor such fines into the costs of doing business.

But perpetrator accountability is not the whole answer for prevention strategies. Many times the abuse is caused by larger, more complicated factors that need to be addressed. Effective prevention strategies in Shama's case, for instance, require that she be provided with training in more marketable skills so that she and her family are not so economically desperate that they need to go to a mudalali. It's also important to establish alternative forms of microcredit for these families so they can get small loans for emergencies or their own means of production without having to go to the mudalali.

Structural prevention often means trying to bring about changes in local or government agencies. We may bring to account the individual police officers operating a brothel of forced prostitution, but if the police leadership is not encouraged and assisted in developing better accountability structures for managing their personnel, then it is likely to happen again. Similarly, we may bring the soldiers of the Lupao massacre to account, but if there is no military training in the proper use of force and no accountability within the command structure, the pressures of combating guerilla warfare are likely to lead to further abuses.

Obviously, the issues of structural prevention are complicated and often require large-scale, long-term remedies, but every individual case of abuse can provide helpful information about the need for and appropriate design of such preventive strategies.

Victim assistance. "He upholds the cause of the oppressed and gives food to the hungry . . . lifts up those who are bowed down . . . watches over the alien and sustains the fatherless and the widow" (Psalm 146:7-9).

As a result of abuse, the victims and their families may need some basic humanitarian assistance. The girls released from forced prostitution are often without families and need shelter and transitional subsistence as well as critical counseling and spiritual care. The widow pushed off her land may need financial assistance until her property is restored to her. The prisoner's family needs to be attended to if the primary breadwinner is incarcerated or injured. The torture victim is likely to need basic medical attention, psychological treatment and spiritual restoration.

The Second Step: Choose the Best Method

After we have determined what type of intervention the victim needs, the next step is to find the *method* of intervention that will work the best. In trying to stop the oppressors (that is, seeking victim rescue, perpetrator accountability or structural prevention), we can choose from seven different approaches. Depending on the situation, we may use these approaches independently, jointly or incrementally. The best method of intervention is based on an analysis of the oppressor's source of power and the limitations of that power.

Method 1: Spiritual intercession. As Christians we readily acknowledge the biblical teachings about the spiritual forces of darkness that often lie behind the evil works of humans (Ephesians 6:12). Thus we engage the spiritual struggle through our prayers in the name of Christ, and through the Spirit who intercedes with God for us (Romans 8:26-27).

God calls on his people to pray about situations of injustice. In praying for the victims, every one of us can participate in what he is doing to help them. In the mysterious ways of God, our prayers—the prayers of the righteous—are "powerful and effective" for all those who are "in trouble" (James 5:13-16). When the Israelites cried out for deliverance from their oppressors in Egypt, God heard their cry and delivered them (Exodus 3:7-9). Again, after the Israelites had entered the Promised Land, they were taken captive and oppressed, but when they asked God for release, he granted it. The Israelites later praised him: "From heaven you heard them ['our forefathers'], and in your great compassion you gave them deliverers, who rescued them from the hand of their oppressors" (Nehemiah 9:27). As David declared, "My prayer is ever against the deeds of evildoers" (Psalm 141:5).

Through our prayer we become spiritually prepared to see the powerful and merciful hand of God. The intercessory prayer ministry of the International Justice Mission finds great inspiration in the wise words of volunteer prayer mentor Vera Shaw:

> As we recognize many cries for justice, we ask: "Who is sufficient for these things?" We're reminded: "Not by might, nor by power, but by my Spirit, says the Lord." With confidence in God, who loves justice and answers prayer, we can reply, "Not that we are sufficient ourselves to think anything of ourselves, but our sufficiency is of God."

For the daily prayer partners of the International Justice Mission, each month brings new testimonies of the faithfulness of God. The case of Samson Gahungu was a thrilling example, for he had been the object of fervent, focused prayer. Like those faithful Christians gathered to pray for Peter in prison (Acts 12), the prayer partners of the International Justice Mission were "overjoyed" and "astonished" to learn of the way God in his sufficiency answered their prayers by releasing Samson from jail.

Of course, our prayers should also lead us into loving action for those who are in need: "Suppose a brother or sister is without clothes and daily food. If one of you says to him, 'Go, I wish you well; keep warm and well fed,' but does nothing about his physical needs, what good is it? In the same way, faith by itself, if it is not accompanied by action, is dead (James 2:15-17). As we are able, we must seek out those practical interventions on behalf of the oppressed that demonstrate our willingness to love not "with words or tongue, but with actions and in truth" (1 John 3:18). For we must remember that *our* obedience is God's plan for answering many prayers of intercession. When the victims of injustice around the world pray as David did, "O righteous God, who searches minds and hearts, bring to an end the violence of the wicked and make the righteous secure," we, God's people, can be the hands through which God intends to answer their prayer (Psalm 7:9).

Method 2: Personal appeal. In some instances oppressors may relent, largely on the power of a personal appeal to their sense of morality, shame, pride, pity or spiritual convictions. We are not speaking here of the nonviolent methods of public civil disobedience or the pressures of public opinion, which can move oppressors to repent of their ways "voluntarily." We will get to these strategies later. Rather this is an appeal made on an individual basis. Once we have all the information about the abuse suffered by the victim, it may be possible to arrange a direct, personal encounter with the one responsible for the oppression and seek his or her help in relieving the suffering. If the oppressor is as good a person as King David, we might, like the prophet Nathan, find wonderful success through such an approach.

Sometimes oppressors do not fully comprehend the consequences of their actions and may change their course of action once they learn of their true impact. I can tell you, for instance, that most white South Africans knew less about the consequences of apartheid for the lives of average black South Africans than a reasonably well-informed American who watched the evening news during that era. It may have been willful ignorance, but for many it was ignorance nonetheless. Consequently, successful efforts at introducing white South Africans to the unspeakable, everyday, real-world suffering of their black neighbors (efforts which the government vigorously opposed) often had a ground-shaking impact on whites. The miraculous way in which white South Africans "gave up" the oppressive (and tremendously profitable) structures of apartheid is largely a testimony of the power of appealing to the better aspects of their nature.[1]

In my experience, personal appeals are most effective in stopping oppression when they are made privately (sparing a public loss of face), on the basis of some personal relationship (with shared spiritual convictions often providing a bridge), in a context in which the oppressing party has not been fully exposed to the way his or her actions affect vulnerable people, and under circumstances where the oppressor is not fundamentally relying on the oppression to sustain a position of power or affluence.

We must have faith in God's capacity to work through his law, which remains stamped on each person's heart—"their consciences also bearing witness, and their thoughts now accusing" (Romans 2:15). And we must be willing to take risks when we sense God leading us in making such personal appeals. On the other hand, Christians, being generally of good will and often unaccustomed to seeing the ugly underbelly of humanity's fallen nature, can easily overestimate the efficacy of such appeals. Most oppressors in this world are not King David. They are more like the pharaoh who was unwilling to release the Hebrews from oppression until God finally took the life of his son—and even so, he later sent his soldiers into the desert to try to slaughter them.

In most cases, therefore, we must press on to consider the other intervention options, which focus on the sources and limitations of oppressors' power.

Method 3: Legal sanction. One of the first questions we must ask after documenting a case of abuse is whether the conduct is illegal according to the country's own laws. If so, we may be able to use the power of law enforcement to bring relief to the victim and accountability to the perpetrators. The trickier question in many cases, however, is whether there is a functional legal system that is accessible to the victims of abuse. Can local law-enforcement authorities be relied on to bring relief? In the developing world where the victims are poor and marginalized, the law-enforcement system tends to be corrupted by money, making it very difficult for those without money to get relief. In the Philippines, for example, the work of prosecuting someone for a crime is not primarily performed by a public prosecutor but by a private prosecutor hired by the victim's family. Obviously if they can't afford to hire such an advocate, they have no guarantee that the case will be vigorously prosecuted—especially if the accused is a person of power and affluence in the community.

The corruption of the legal process can be even more obvious. In Bombay, for instance, International Justice Mission researchers could openly observe police officers in the area making their rounds to the brothels to collect their *hafta*—monthly bribe. Working the red-light district in Bombay is so profitable for police officers that they actually bribe their own commanders in order to gain the privilege of being assigned to the district. If a police officer is on the brothel pay roll, how likely is that officer to lead raids on it to rescue children? Similarly, holding someone in bonded servitude may be illegal in India, but this doesn't stop people from enslaving at least 15 million children. Obviously the problem lies not so much with the law but with its enforcement.

We can, however, overcome these obstacles. To the extent that the victim's poverty is a problem, Christians can provide funds or professional services to ensure vigorous legal representation. To put it bluntly, in systems where money indirectly buys justice, Christians (especially wealthy Western Christians) can secure justice for the oppressed by paying for or helping provide vigorous legal representation.

We can get around the general corruption of the law-enforcement system if we take the time to find the exception to the rule—the honest and committed officials—because they are frequently there to be found. A general lack of the enforcement of laws against bonded labor may prevail in India, but the International Justice Mission has seen hundreds of children released from bonded labor and hundreds of mudalalis arrested because we have funneled our investigative work through a highly committed magistrate (who happens to be a Christian) who enforces the law. Likewise, in Bombay the International Justice Mission has established a relationship with a police commander of exceptional integrity who will conduct raids with us on brothels to release children we have identified as abducted. So if we don't mind the credit for our efforts going to local law enforcement, we can take advantage of some very fruitful opportunities for legal-sanction interventions through indigenous authorities.

In any case, if the oppressive conduct uncovered by our investigation is illegal, then we should seek to limit the oppressor's power by getting the state to enforce the law. Thus the focused strategy becomes a question of accessing the legal system and bringing the coercive power of the state to bear on the side of the victim.

Method 4: Command discipline. As noted in the discussion of coercion in chapter nine, most of those who actually carry out the exercise of coercive force are usually sent by someone else and thus are part of a chain of command. This is most obviously true for police and soldiers. Theoretically they carry the implements of coercive force only because they are authorized to do so by the state. Also in theory they are authorized to use this coercive force only under a very limited set of circumstances and subject to the commands of their superiors. The government gives soldiers and police guns, but they are only authorized to use them when the law says they can and only when their superiors allow them to. So while burly soldiers and police carrying guns often look like they wield tremendous power, usually they are simply the tools of other people and exercise very limited power themselves.

In cases of abuse by the police and military, then, the individuals involved are usually either exercising their force outside the limits of their commander's orders or outside the limits of the law. The police abducting girls into a brothel, for instance, are exercising their coercive force not only outside the law, but probably outside their commander's orders—at least their most senior commanders. Thus they are operating as common criminals. Their status as police should offer them no protection. Sometimes at a lower level of the chain of command, their immediate supervisors will protect them—out of loyalty, corruption or mutual protection. Then we must simply find a place high enough in the chain of command to make our intervention.

I know of very few places in the world, for instance, where, if we had video footage of officers running a brothel with children, we would be unable to get assistance from the highest level of the police command—the key being the investigative product that makes doubts about the officers' involvement impossible. Even the most corrupt police commander, if senior enough, would rather cashier a few low-level police officers rather than suffer the embarrassment of being seen to openly countenance forced prostitution of children. The commander can take away their instruments of coercive force and their authority to exercise force (by dismissing them from their job), and can subject them to the same legal sanctions that a common criminal would face. So the challenge is to effectively target our intervention at the proper level of the chain of command.

Likewise, the soldiers who seized Samson Gahungu and held him prisoner may seem intimidating, but they are only doing the bidding of the leaders of the military regime. Intervention, then, needs to be made with the supreme authorities of the regime; if successful, Samson will be released by those soldiers as quickly as he was whisked off the street. An understanding of the chain of command helps us focus our intervention analysis not on the soldiers and police but on those who command them. As the Roman centurion told Jesus: "For I myself am a man under authority, with soldiers under me. I tell this one, 'Go,' and he goes; and that one, 'Come,' and he comes. I say to my servant, 'Do this,' and he does it" (Matthew 8:9).

Even when soldiers and police are operating out of control, the focus of our intervention will still be on their superiors in the chain of command, who have, after all, equipped the rogue individuals with the instruments and authority of force. If the investigation proves that the abuse is taking place by police or soldiers, the chain of command will be an important intervention asset.

More serious difficulties arise when the abusive police or soldiers are conducting their abuses within the law of the country. Some countries—like Israel, for instance—do not prohibit all torture during interrogation. When I lived in South Africa, it was not illegal to detain someone without charge or trial. It was technically illegal to torture them, but it was tolerated and even ordered by commanders of the security forces. Under these circumstances, interventions within the chain of command will generally not be effective. So we use a different strategy of intervention, one that takes into account the sources and limitations of the government's power.

Method 5: Public shame. When the government authorities are unwilling to stop the abuse through domestic legal sanctions or unwilling to bring the perpetrators to account through its chain of command, then advocates for the victims must intervene through other means. If the Philippine government, for instance, is unwilling to bring to justice the soldiers who perpetrated the Lupao massacre through its own court-martial system, then other measures must be considered. If the military regime in Nigeria is unwilling to cease the detention and torture of political dissidents, then other methods must be considered for bringing power to bear on the side of the victims.

One way to devise such an intervention strategy is to consider the government's own sources of power and its dependent relationships. Governments and authorities can always *look* very powerful, but their power is always derivative—it's derived from relationships with other people, institutions and resources. Who do the leaders of this country depend on for their power to rule? Do they rule because of their popularity and legitimacy among the people of the country? Do they rule by the force of arms; if so, how do they pay for their guns and their soldiers? Do they depend on economic relationships with major corporations or other governments?

If a government rules significantly because of its popularity or legitimacy with the country's broader public, then one of the most powerful ways to intervene on behalf of the victims of abuse is through an appeal to the public. Thus effective efforts at publicizing the documented abuses through the media, public demonstrations, educational events and conferences can cause the government to lose its popularity and legitimacy among the people that it depends on to rule.

President Aquino, in the Philippines, was very sensitive to public opinion, especially on human-rights matters. Thus she would be very sensitive to a broad public outcry over the Lupao massacre. In President Aquino's case, however, it was discovered that she did not rule purely because of popular support but largely because a significant block of the nation's military leaders *allowed* her to rule. Since this was the case, if those military leaders didn't want to bring the Lupao massacre perpetrators to justice, then an appeal to President Aquino through popular opinion may not work.

Discovering that the government's power rests with military leaders rather than popularly elected civilian leadership requires a shift in intervention strategy. The focus must turn to the dependent relationships of the military leaders. Among other things, we may find that these leaders depend heavily on relationships with foreign governments for funds, arms, legitimacy or economic prosperity. In the case of the Philippines there was a strong relationship between the military and the United States government. Knowing this, we might bring the information about the Lupao massacre to the attention of U.S. government authorities so that they might use their influence with the Philippine military leaders—through the State Department, congressional inquiries, the U.S.'s presence at the United Nations and so on. Of course, if U.S. government leaders do not wish to act on behalf of the victims of Lupao, then the case can be taken to the relationships that those leaders depend on, that is, the U.S. government leaders' relationships with the American public.

Observing this chain of dependent relationships, we can see the various points at which it is possible to intervene with the documented evidence of the abuse. Seeing how this chain of relationships works explains why it might be extremely important that documented evidence of events in a little village in a country of southeast Asia reaches the eyes and ears of a caring American public. A lot of rulers and authorities around the world depend quite heavily on their relationship with the only remaining superpower on the globe—the United States—and its corporations. There was a significant change, for instance, in the U.S. government's willingness to support the military leaders in El Salvador when it became clear that the military had been connected to the rape and murder of a number of Catholic nuns.

Thus effective intervention on behalf of the victims of abuse can come from subjecting the authorities to public shame for their failure to stop the abuses or their failure to bring the perpetrators to justice. This intervention can be effective not only because the rulers cannot afford to look bad in front of the people they depend on, but also because governments really do prefer to be viewed as legitimate governments rather than as criminals. Recall that when it comes to the use of coercive force, the only thing that separates government authorities from common criminals is the legitimacy, lawfulness or proper authority they claim for the force that they use. Therefore, if we can publicly demonstrate that a government's use of force was unlawful or without legitimacy, many governments will make efforts to amend their ways. Of course many will amend their ways simply by making it harder to find out what it is they are doing, but that is an investigative question, not an intervention question. On the other hand, if we have the documented information that *proves* the government's exercise of force was illegitimate, then we may have powerful ammunition for intervening on the victim's behalf.

A government's sensitivity to questions of legitimacy is one reason why international law (like the Universal Declaration of Human Rights or the Geneva Conventions) and international institutions (like the United Nations and the United Nation's Human Rights Committee) are so important. It's not so much that the system of international law and the United Nations have effective instruments for enforcing international codes of conduct, because for the most part they don't.[2] Rather, they provide objective standards against which the actions of governments can be measured. We can look to the language about the sanctity of religious freedom in the Universal Declaration of Human Rights—which almost every country has signed—and say to Saudi Arabia or China or Cuba: "By standards that you yourself have agreed to, your treatment of Christians or other religious minorities is 'illegitimate' and has no 'proper authority' and is therefore criminal."

Moreover, the international system not only provides standards but organizations like the United Nations and the U.N. Human Rights Committee also provide a forum through which information about abuses can be publicized—thoughtfully and broadly. When the Soviet Union shot down a Korean airliner years ago, every nation was forced to see all the facts as they were presented before the United Nations. We can have tremendous facts of abuse, but if we don't have a forum to publicize it—and a forum that both our friends and enemies have to listen to—then our facts may do us no good.

The effect of public and international opinion can be very powerful. Its effectiveness can be vastly overestimated, but public shame can be a forceful ally on the side of vulnerable, powerless victims of oppression. And as Nathan the prophet knows, there is nothing ungodly about presenting the facts of abuse boldly and truthfully before rulers and the public; it is an act of courageous love on behalf of those who are victimized by the abuse of authority. Conversely, we learn from Jonah's story that there are circumstances under which the failure to speak the truth to abusive and sinful rulers is an act of sin, of open rebellion against God.

Method 6: Economic interventions. Under circumstances in which the oppressive leaders seem impervious to the powers of public shame, we may consider forceful interventions of power on behalf of the victims. Frequently an analysis of the oppressor's sources of power and dependent relationships leads us to consider methods of intervention that affect the oppressors' economic interests.

The military rulers of Nigeria in recent years, for instance, did not seem to mind being viewed as criminal thugs by much of the world. They went about executing their critics, torturing their political prisoners, stealing their country's public wealth—all the while largely remaining unimpressed by the verbal condemnations of the United

Nations and various national governments. As the U.S. State Department bluntly described conditions in Nigeria in 1997: "All branches of the security forces committed serious human rights abuses. . . . Security forces continued to commit extrajudicial killings and use excessive force to quell antigovernment protests. . . . Security forces tortured and beat suspects and detainees."[3]

The United Nations Human Rights Committee articulated its concerns about Nigeria this way:

> The Committee is deeply concerned by the high number of extra-judicial and summary executions, disappearances, cases of torture, ill-treatment and arbitrary arrest and detention by members of the army and security forces and by the failure of the government to investigate fully these cases, to prosecute alleged offences, to punish those found guilty and provide compensation to the victims or their families. The resulting state of impunity encourages further violations of Covenant rights.[4]

The heads of state of the Commonwealth countries were meeting in New Zealand in 1995 and threatened to expel Nigeria from the Commonwealth if it proceeded with the execution of nine prominent political dissidents. The Nigerian government killed them all anyway. The Human Rights Watch reported: "Africa's most populous country [Nigeria] became a full-fledged human rights outlaw in 1995."[5]

Clearly the power of public shame was insufficient to protect the victims of the Nigerian government's abuse of power. So we must ask, What is the source of the government's power? What relationships does it depend on to maintain its rule? It's safe to say that the Nigerian military government remained in power through the force of its military and the support of a ruling clique that siphons off the country's natural resources for handsome profits. Of course to pay for this military force and these powerful friends, the rulers needed money. And where did they get their money? Over 80 percent of the military regime's revenues come from the sale of oil—about ten billion dollars a year. Close to half of that is purchased by Americans at the gas pump, especially through Shell Oil. If the military regime were seriously threatened with an end to its oil revenues, they might not be so cavalier about the way they go about the brutal abuse of power.

The suggestion here is that it is possible under certain circumstances to intervene on behalf of the victims of injustice by creating negative economic consequences for the perpetrators. The economic sanctions imposed on South Africa are often cited as having applied constructive pressure upon the government for change. Similarly, economic sanctions have been suggested for countries engaged in the persecution of Christians—Sudan, China, Cuba and others.

A number of problems arise, however, when we consider imposing economic sanctions on abusive governments. Sanctions may further isolate a rogue regime from any moderating contact with other nations. Many times the common people are hurt by the sanctions while the ruling clique continues to prosper. Often some other countries will simply replace whatever economic partnerships other countries have withdrawn. Finally, if not surgically targeted at the point of true economic vulnerability for the oppressors, the impact of the sanctions will be defused throughout the society and prove ineffective.

Nevertheless, oppressive powers do have economic vulnerabilities, and occasionally they can be powerfully influenced by a thoughtful and consistent combination of pressures, including economic pressures. This can be particularly true for economic actors that may have oppressive practices. American-owned shoe manufacturers, for instance, have begun to take serious steps to address some of the abusive child-labor conditions of their overseas suppliers because of the economic threat they see in being associated with the oppressive "sweatshop" suffering of children. Likewise, countries in Asia have come to be concerned about the effect on vital international tourist dollars if their leaders are perceived as turning a blind eye to the brutalities of child prostitution.

Method 7: Military force. Under the most extreme circumstances where the oppressor cannot be influenced by the pressures of public shame or negative economic consequences and where the quality and magnitude of human rights abuses is extraordinarily grave, then military force may be considered as a tool of intervention on behalf of the oppressed. There are, of course, numerous complications that accompany the decision of one country to intervene militarily in the affairs of another country, and some Christians from the peace church tradition would oppose the use of such force under any circumstances.

I, on the other hand, believe that there are a limited number of opportunities in which the use of military force can be effective and godly. I believe that short of military force, there would have been no other way to stop Hitler's slaughter of the Jews in Europe. More recently, a consensus of 20/20 hindsight has been reached in American foreign policy circles that the United Nations or powerful Western nations could have saved hundreds of thousands of lives in Rwanda through a brief and overwhelming deployment of military force. Such a deployment would not have solved Rwanda's long-term problems of ethnic violence, but it could have quickly brought to a halt the orgy of genocidal murder that saw perhaps half a million people butchered by machetes.

The dynamics of international military police action is far too complex to discuss here, but suffice it to say that there are times when a loving response to the victims of the world's most horrendous and determined oppressors requires prayerful consideration of forceful action.

The Third Step: Determine the Most Effective Agent
Finally, when we have carefully chosen the most appropriate type of

intervention and the most promising method of intervention, we must wisely consider the best *agent* of intervention. The type of intervention tells us *what kind* of relief to seek. The method tells us *how* to seek it. Questions about the *agent* of change focus our attention on *who* should be the one to implement the intervention strategy. To determine the best choice, we can ask five pertinent questions.

1. Who is in the most secure position to seek the intervention? Those who intervene on behalf of the oppressed frequently face risks of retaliation, but not everyone faces the same level of risk. As a foreigner from the United States, I was in a much safer position to ask the Philippine Army hard questions about the Lupao massacre than were the vulnerable villagers. Occasionally it may be safer to funnel a Christian ministry's information about abuses through a well-known, indigenous advocacy group in a way that does not draw unwanted attention to the expatriate Christian ministry. Also a prominent leader of high social standing may be less vulnerable to recrimination than an impoverished and vulnerable squatter—and thus might be a more secure agent of intervention.

2. Who will have the most efficient and effective access to the people with whom the intervention is targeted? The variety of intervention types and methods may require access to the courts, to government leaders, to international organizations, to the media, to social and economic elites, and so on. Consequently, it is worth considering the different kinds of people who might gain quickest access to the targeted audience.

3. Who has the best relationship or basis for a relationship with the people whose assistance is most critical for the intervention? The intervention generally requires not only access to the right people but also some level of cooperation from these individuals. Such cooperation is most likely to come from people who connect at a personal level because they share common backgrounds, interests or communities.

4. Who has the expertise that is required? There are some interventions that require a specific expertise. Courtroom interventions are generally limited to practicing lawyers. Media and public relations interventions require yet another set of skills. Interventions with the United Nations and other international bodies also may require a specific expertise. Obviously, when choosing an agent for a specialized intervention, we should choose one with the appropriate expertise.

5. Who has the greatest credibility? The agent of the intervention must have credibility with the one to whom the intervention is targeted. The sources of personal credibility vary; they frequently include the elements mentioned above—preexisting relationships, job specialty, expertise. But credibility also may be a matter of political background, ideological tradition, family background, social status, ethnicity and professional or educational background. Evaluating the relevant personal credibility factors will help us choose the best agent for the intervention.

In all these matters, as we try to obey God's call to intervene on behalf of the oppressed, we will surely need his wisdom and guidance. As Jesus advised his disciples when facing abusive officials, we must be "as shrewd as snakes and as innocent as doves" (Matthew 10:16). Fortunately, God *promises* to grant us wisdom if we only ask him for it in faith (James 1:5). May he then grant us the wisdom to pursue the appropriate type of intervention, the best method and the most effective agent as we rescue victims of abuse.

Twelve

The Body of Christ in Action

What We All Can Do

G OD IS IN THE BUSINESS OF USING THE UNLIKELY TO PER-form the holy. To declare his glory God worked through an old man with few relatives and no children and established a nation whose descendants would outnumber the stars, and through whom "all peoples on earth will be blessed" (Genesis 12:3; 15:5). To slay an oppressive giant who terrorized entire armies of Israel, God worked through a scrawny shepherd boy who didn't even know how to dress for battle. To build the church of Jesus Christ and to turn the world upside down, God worked through the most unlikely crew of humble women and common fishermen—not many wise, not many powerful, not many noble (1 Corinthians 1:26).

We Are All Qualified to Seek Justice

God is in the business of using the "foolish" and the "weak" to accomplish his divine will on earth, and that simply means that I am qualified to be on his team. We all are. And when it comes to seeking justice for the hurting in our world, he doesn't have a special roster.

He intends to use you and me. He doesn't have any other plan. In fact, it was precisely for such good works that we were created; they don't save us or make us righteous before God, but they allow us to fulfill the godly purpose for which God created us. As Paul wrote, "For we are God's workmanship, created in Christ Jesus to do good works, which God prepared in advance for us to do" (Ephesians 2:10). And what are *good* works? "He has told you, O mortal, what is *good;* and what does the LORD require of you but to do justice, and to love kindness, and to walk humbly with your God?" (Micah 6:8 NRSV). Again, when the prophet Isaiah tells us to "learn to *do good,*" he follows with the more specific exhortation to "seek justice, rescue the oppressed, defend the orphan, plead for the widow" (Isaiah 1:17 NRSV).

When it comes to seeking justice in a world of vulnerable men, women and children, all of us are privileged to play a role. As with all of the good works at the core of God's priorities, this is an all-hands-on-deck proposition. When it comes to sharing the good news of Jesus Christ, for example, all of us do what we can. Some of us will preach to stadiums full of people, some will translate the Scriptures for a whole language group, some will stand and give a testimony to a sparsely attended prayer breakfast and others will share their faith over a cup of coffee with a friend. Still others will support each of these endeavors with prayers, financial resources or simple words of encouragement. But *all* of God's people are privileged to "give a reason for the hope" that is in them and can do *something* to advance Christ's commission to make disciples among all the nations (1 Peter 3:15).

Our calling does not stop with sharing the good news. *All* of us are also called to do *something* to care for the poor. If we aren't, then, asks the apostle John, how can the love of God be within us? (1 John 3:17). And we are *all* called to do *something* to seek justice for the oppressed. Why? Because along with mercy and faith, justice, Jesus said, is one of the "more important matters," one that none of us can neglect (Matthew 23:23).

Besides, why would we want to neglect it? We would miss out on the many opportunities to express our love for God and for our neighbors. In so doing, we also would miss out on the fullness that God intended for our life. For this is, after all, the "abundant" life for which Christ came to earth and died for us—a life of godly significance, of divine importance (John 10:10 NRSV).

Truly we can't share the gospel with everyone, feed all the hungry, comfort all the afflicted or rescue all the oppressed, but *all* of us can, praise God, do *something* to advance these priorities of God. There certainly are different seasons of activity, different gifts and different needs and opportunities in the life of a follower of Christ, but if we ever look at the works that God asks us to do—proclaim the gospel, help the poor, defend the abused—and say, "Well, you know, that's really not *my* thing," then we have simply made a conscious decision to impoverish our spiritual life. Christ in his holiness abhors injustice. As we grow into his character and image, we not only grow in our passion to seek justice, we are also led into those concrete good works for which we were created.

Each member of the body of Christ has a very tangible role; Christ in his grace has shut *none* of us out of his glory. Clearly, not everyone has the same role, and an appreciation of the special gifts and expertise that God has granted for the work is extremely important. But Christ accepts every offering and often counts the most humble offering as the greatest.

Seeking justice is the task of bringing truth and power to bear on behalf of those who are oppressed, and here the diverse gifts of the body are called out in glorious array.

Shepherds and Teachers

It may surprise some, but perhaps the most crucial task rests with the shepherds and teachers of the body of Christ—those who help us know God. Our engagement with the work of justice is no more and no less than an extension of our desire to follow our God and Savior. Thus the entire army of God can remain disengaged from the battle if they do not know enough about their Lord to hear his voice. Or worse, they can be led off into a passionate struggle for justice following only the carnal call of men, a struggle that ends up knowing only the voice of raw power. But if our leaders—the pastors, seminary professors, ministry trainers, Sunday-school teachers, Bible-study leaders and educators of our churches and organizations—teach us about the God of justice, we can, and will, follow *him* in the struggle against injustice.

That is the role of shepherds and teachers. They will lead us in the authority of the Word of God to know God's passion for justice, Christ's compassion for the oppressed, God's holy condemnation of the sinful abuse of power and his deep desire to rescue the vulnerable. From the Word of God our teachers will show us that God's plan for seeking justice in the world is to use his people to work acts of love and rescue. Our teachers will equip us with a hope that will withstand the inevitable trials and suffering that accompany obedience to Christ. Our teachers will prepare us to be witnesses for Christ's love and holiness in a hurting world of oppression.

Or—they won't.

Some teachers will be so shocked by the unfamiliarity of this God of justice, that they will, like the Pharisees of Jesus' day, return to a rigorous and passionate worship of a different God—their familiar God of tithes and sacrifices—and neglect the God of the Bible, the God of justice, mercy and faith. What a heavy responsibility and glorious opportunity is in the hands of Christian teachers. Jesus called the teachers and guides of his own people back to their Scriptures, to rediscover this God who had become unknown to them. At least one teacher came secretly to Jesus in the night to learn more (John 3:1-17), but most teachers simply grew angry at the suggestion that they had veered from the God of the Scriptures. They closed their ears to the voice of Christ.

Others leaders and teachers, however, will, like Saul of Tarsus, hear Jesus. They will see that even in their zealousness to serve God, they have missed out on a full knowledge of him. The Scriptures will come alive for them with a freshness that they have not known in years. They will rediscover Christ's simple and straightforward proclamation:

> The Spirit of the Lord is on me,
>> because he has anointed me
>> to preach good news to the poor.
> He has sent me to proclaim freedom for the prisoners
>> and recovery of sight for the blind,
>> to release the oppressed,
> to proclaim the year of the Lord's favor. (Luke 4:18)

Yes Christ has come to set us free from sin and death through his sacrifice on the cross, but he has also come to deliver the poor, the prisoner and the oppressed. The prophet Isaiah made this clear to the leaders of Israel who were tiring God out with their prayer meetings and their spectacles of fasting in sackcloth and ashes.

> Is not this the kind of fasting I have chosen:
> to loose the chains of injustice,
>> and untie the cords of the yoke,
> to set the oppressed free,
>> and break every yoke?
> Is it not to share your food with the hungry
>> and to provide the poor wanderer with shelter—
> when you see the naked, to clothe him,
>> and not to turn away from your own flesh and blood?
>>> (Isaiah 58:6-7)

"*Then,*" says the prophet,

> your light will break forth like the dawn,

and your healing will quickly appear;
then your righteousness will go before you,
   the glory of the LORD will be your rear guard.
Then you will call, and the LORD will answer;
   you will cry for help, and he will say: Here am I.
      (Isaiah 58:8-9)

The teachers and shepherds of today's church have a huge task before them in helping Christians come to know the God of justice. Our Bible scholars, theologians and historians need to dig deeply into the Scriptures to help us understand how God in his holiness relates to the sinful abuse of power and how we can do our part in "setting the oppressed free." In the twentieth century we grew in our understanding of evangelism, world missions, care for the poor, healing of the sick. We also learned how to be a voice of moral integrity within an idolatrous and promiscuous society. But we have a wonderful journey ahead of us in understanding a Christian's role in a world where power is used to abuse the weak. And the body of Christ cannot take up its rightful ministry of justice if its mind has not been thoroughly renewed by and rooted in the Word of God.

Thus every pastor, professor, scholar, Sunday-school teacher and Bible-study leader has a tangible place to start: searching the Word of God to know the God of justice.

The LORD will guide you always;
   he will satisfy your needs in a sun-scorched land
   and will strengthen your frame.
You will be like a well-watered garden,
   Like a spring whose waters never fail.
Your people will rebuild the ancient ruins
   and will raise up the age-old foundations;
you will be called Repairer of Broken Walls,
   Restorer of Streets with Dwellings. (Isaiah 58:11-12)

Frontline Global Workers

The next most critical role in developing a Christian witness for justice in the world will be played by frontline workers in the field—the tens of thousands of missionaries and relief and development workers that minister throughout the world. After all, they represent the very incarnation of the body of Christ within the communities where the victims of abuse actually live. Living and working among the poor, the marginalized, the minorities and the isolated peoples of our world, these frontline workers are the eyes and ears of the body of Christ. They hear from the prisoner's family after their father is dragged away by security forces. They notice—as few others do—when little girls disappear, having been abducted into sexual exploitation. The widow dispossessed of her land is actually a member of their congregation. The minority tribal group members being harassed by the army are the people for whom the missionary has been translating the Scriptures. The missionary doctor is the one who stitches the wounds of the student tortured by the police. The child sold into bonded labor or raped by a town councilor is actually a sponsored child of the Christian relief and development agency.

It's fair to say that within a stone's throw of just about every victim of oppression in the world there is a Christian worker whom God has called and placed in the community to share the love of Jesus.

Remember that the key to oppressors' power over victims is to isolate them from those who might be able to intervene on their behalf. As long as victims are cut off from those who might be able to expose oppressors' deceptions and introduce a counteracting power to protect the victims, oppressors are free to abuse the weak. God's first step in enabling the body of Christ to seek justice for the oppressed, therefore, has been to break down the isolation of the vulnerable by deploying his witnesses into their communities—into every city, village, hamlet, nook and cranny of this broad world. What an amazing thing God has done through those who have obeyed the call of Christ to international service! He has sent his disciples into the far reaches of the world, and the oppressed are not alone.

Why Missionaries Often Can't Directly Intervene

Many Christians are tempted to make the mistake, however, of expecting these global workers to provide direct intervention on behalf of the victims of abuse. In many cases this is unwise. As we have seen, seeking justice for such victims requires overcoming the oppressor's powers of deception and coercion through a careful investigation of the facts and a tactical intervention with appropriate authorities. Taking on such a task requires a number of resources that, in my experience, global Christian workers are already in short supply.

1. Emotional energy. Taking on the cause of a victim of abuse requires substantial emotional energy as you interact with the victim's pain and the relentless frustrations of seeking vindication for their cause. The emotional drain of it all can quickly run a missionary down, and if he or she starts the process with depleted emotional resources, it's very difficult to persevere.

2. Time. A careful accounting of the facts and a persistent intervention with authorities can require extensive expenditures of time. Stepping with conviction into the complicated and frustrating world of the oppressed, a global worker can find many days swallowed up by the endeavor.

3. Finances. These efforts can also require significant expenditures of financial resources. To ministries already feeling the strain of limited funds, the expenses that accompany a proper investigation and intervention can prove a great burden.

4. Security. Most critically, perhaps, intervention on behalf of a victim requires a certain level of security against personal or governmental retaliation. As guests in a foreign country global Christian workers are particularly vulnerable to governmental retaliation if the authorities are unhappy with the questions workers are asking or the cause they are pleading. The trouble-making worker or ministry can be kicked out of the country. Necessary permits or licenses can be denied. Legal and civil protections or privileges can be withdrawn. Worse, missionary workers who live *in* the community may be vulnerable to personal, physical retaliation from the oppressive forces in the community.

5. Expertise. Most global Christian workers simply don't have the expertise that these cases require. Very few missionaries or relief and development workers have professional backgrounds in criminal investigation, risk assessment, legal intervention, government relations and other areas of expertise that are frequently required in such matters.

Thus when the special needs of abused children, widows, prisoners or refugees come to their attention, these workers are generally not in a very strong position to directly intervene on their behalf. Nor is it fair to expect them to do so in most cases. The victim of oppression is worthy of the expenditure of emotional energy, time, resources, personal security and expertise that their cause requires, but it does not follow that, in the fullness of the body of Christ, all of this should fall on our frontline workers in the field—workers, who for the most part have been sent and equipped for very different tasks. When the missionary who teaches theology at the Bible school in Ethiopia starts to see signs of famine in the community, we don't expect him to become an expert in emergency humanitarian relief. When the church planter in Southeast Asia finds mounting conditions of drought, we usually don't expect her to become a hydraulic engineer. When a woman in the village needs cataract surgery, we don't expect the Bible translator to do it. Rather in each case we look to the broader body of Christ and call on the surgeons, the well drillers and the famine fighters.

We can rightly expect the missionary at the seminary to share some rice with a next-door neighbor. We might expect the church planter to teach the villagers about boiling water. And we might expect the Bible translator to bandage a simple wound. Similarly, on occasion international workers will be in a reasonable position to seek justice for a victim of abuse in their community and can make a contribution toward the elimination of oppressive conditions. But we are mistaken if we think that seeking justice—overcoming coercion and deception—is a simple task that the average caring person is equipped to do. This is simply not the case, and we should adjust our expectations for global Christian workers accordingly.

However, we should not make the mistake of thinking that just because the Christian worker in the field can't do what is required in a given case that there isn't anyone in the body of Christ who can. There will be occasions when there is nothing *anyone* can do, but we must not confuse this very narrow category of cases with the broader category of cases in which there is nothing that the *fieldworker* can do. Between the list of cases where *no one* can help and the list of cases where the *fieldworker* cannot help is a long list of cases where *someone* can help. The average fieldworker, for example, stands utterly powerless before the elderly woman in the community who has grown blind from cataracts. But for the Christian surgeon, a miraculous healing of her sight is just a routine surgery away. Likewise, the case of injustice that seems utterly helpless to the fieldworker may be a rather straightforward piece of work to a Christian public justice professional.

What we need, then, is to make sure that global Christian workers have access to such resources and expertise. We must ensure that the full body of Christ is tending to the needs of the world rather than piling yet another unfair burden on missionaries and relief and development workers.

So What *Can* Fieldworkers Do?
International Christian workers can do a great deal: they can share

what they know with the larger body of Christ. The body of Christ depends on the Bible teacher in Ethiopia to tell the story of starvation in the community. The Bible translator must call for the doctor. The church planter must share the need for a new water supply with a development agency that can do something about it.

Of course, these workers must share with the body of Christ the stories of oppression and abuse that they hear and see in their community. This is a three-step task.

1. Fieldworkers should develop the eyes to see and ears to hear about injustice in their community. Jesus is sensitive to the abuse of power among his people, so global Christian workers need to ask God for Christ's tenderness. By conversation and demeanor they will convey to their community that they are interested in listening with a careful ear to the injustice that their neighbors endure. Or they will give the impression that such matters really aren't their concern. In many communities the most powerful way to heed the biblical injunction to bear each other's burdens is to hear the stories of those who are burdened by the oppressive abuse of power (Galatians 6:2). With love and courage these Christian workers can communicate to their neighbors that stories of injustice are of urgent, passionate concern to God and therefore of compelling interest to God's people.

2. Fieldworkers can aid these victims of abuse by helping them to articulate their story. This provides the beginning of a chronicle that others can act on. Workers can do their part to "rescue the oppressed, defend the orphan and plead for the widow" simply by getting out a piece of paper and making some notes about the story. They generally will ask the following questions, trying to elicit answers that are as precise as possible.

□ What is the nature of the injury? How has the victim been hurt? Is the abuse ongoing?

□ Who is the victim?

□ What is the means or method of abuse or injury? How, when and where did the oppressor carry out this injury or abuse?

☐ Who is the perpetrator, and why does he or she commit the abuse?

☐ Is the person who actually performs the abuse sent by someone else or under a chain of command or authority? If so, who is the oppressor's commander or sponsor?

☐ Does the oppressor or the oppressor's commander or sponsor claim some kind of legitimacy or lawful authority for the abuse? What is the basis for such a claim? Are the oppressor's actions legal in the society?

In getting the answers for as many of these questions as possible, the worker should also ask, How do we know the answers to each of these questions? Is it secondhand or thirdhand knowledge, or are these facts established by firsthand accounts or documents or physical evidence? By making such a record the worker will have an essential and powerful tool that others can use to seek intervention for the victim.

3. Fieldworkers need to tell the story. The fieldworkers need to be responsible stewards of the burden that has been shared with them by passing it along carefully to those who might come to the victim's aid. Workers might know people in the community—civic leaders, lawyers or advocates—who could investigate the matter and help the one who is suffering abuse. Sometimes workers don't know whom to turn to with the information, and in some situations turning to the wrong person might have dire consequences. The International Justice Mission has been established specifically for this purpose: to provide global ministries with a Christian agency to whom they can entrust their stories. The International Justice Mission will consult with the ministry about where to turn, or will take on the matter as a case referral and independently pursue an investigation and intervention on behalf of the victim.

Fieldworkers can also share these stories with the churches and individuals that support them back home. Mobilizing the full body of Christ as a witness for justice in the world can only happen when

Christians come to know the heart of their God—the God of justice—and when they come to understand something of the needs around the world. Rather than being bombarded with an overwhelming and unwieldy mass of information about injustice in the world from remote and secular sources, churches and ministry partners can come to see a world of need through the eyes of their fieldworkers in a way that is eminently credible and compelling. No sources are more qualified to provide such a ministry to a church community than the workers they have sent into the field.

In taking these three basic steps fieldworkers love their neighbors as the Good Samaritan did. You will recall that the Good Samaritan's great act of love consisted of three parts (Luke 10:25-37). First, he refused to walk obliviously on the other side of the road when he encountered the injured man; he got close enough to assess the man's needs. Second, he offered what aid he could by bandaging him and taking him to an inn. Third, he referred his hurting neighbor to the innkeeper—a professional who was equipped to meet the man's needs in a way that the Samaritan could not. The Good Samaritan was *good* not because he was able to meet all of the hurting man's needs but because he had mercy on the man, cared for him and then referred him to someone else who could help him.

Global Christian workers can obey Christ and tangibly love their neighbors who suffer abuse by turning compassionate eyes and ears toward them, listening to them, recording their story, and referring them to local or international entities that might help them.

Country and Culture Experts

Apart from its frontline workers in the field, the Christian agencies of world missions and international relief and development have also developed the most extraordinary body of experts on countries and cultures around the world. Name a nationality, an ethnic group, a language group or any other cultural or political subdivision of humanity around the world, and we can find a Christian scholar, researcher or fieldworker who has spent the better part of a lifetime studying their history, culture, mores, traditions, communal dynamics, governance, social systems, religion, worldview, language and leadership.

Over the last few generations the leaders of international missions have committed vast amounts of resources to the study of various countries and cultures. The theory of modern missions in the past couple of generations has focused on the task of conveying the gospel to communities in forms that are readily accessible to the existing culture. The notion of Western missionaries seeing themselves as purveyors of Western culture was abandoned long ago.[1] Instead, Western missionaries have largely come to see themselves as students of the culture into which they enter. And in the educational and training institutions of the church and the missions community worldwide, this study has reached a level of sophistication, comprehensiveness and depth that rivals or exceeds the expertise of secular educational institutions, foreign policy institutions, governmental agencies and international business groups.

As with any community, on occasion the crosscultural scholarship is warped by ideology or personal eccentricities, but in general, if I wanted to know something about the people, society and cultural of Mongolia, Sri Lanka, Kazakstan, Sierra Leone, Paraguay, Iran or Afghanistan, I'd rather have access to the corporate expertise of the networks of Christian mission and crosscultural service than access to the U.S. Foreign Service, the Johns Hopkins School for Advanced International Studies, the Harvard Center for Middle Eastern Studies or the international offices of American Express. Of course, if I could, I'd like to have access to their research, wisdom and experience as well. And the glory of it all is that frequently I can. Burrowed within such secular institutions are yet more Christians whom God has given extraordinary expertise in various cultures.

All of this intelligence and expertise within the worldwide Christian community is tremendously helpful in seeking justice where needed. The experience and know-how of fellow Christians in the practical matters regarding access to a country, logistics, security, geography, transportation and language can be indispensable for conducting investigations and interventions. Particularly when it comes to making interventions, the cultural, social and political expertise and relationships of the broad body of Christ can be extraordinarily helpful. An analysis of a society's power structure, communal dynamics, cultural sensitivities and historical context is extremely important for the development of a surgical and effective intervention, and much of this analysis is readily available within the networks of Christian agencies and institutions.

When the International Justice Mission takes on a case in Manila, India, Chiapas or Bujumbura, it immediately begins to access its networks of country and cultural expertise in the body of Christ. These experts come from mission agencies, universities, governmental agencies, businesses, think tanks, politics—and the list goes on. They help us reach a quick, but in-depth, analysis that might take another human-rights agency years, or generations, to develop. These consultations provide intelligence on the broadest sociopolitical structures and trends within the nation as well as the minutest details of village-level history, politics and culture.

In the Philippines the International Justice Mission may have an organizational chart of the Philippine government, but a Christian executive who has been doing business with that country for fifteen years might help us understand who *really* makes things happen in a certain sphere. In Kenya we might not readily understand how using an interpreter from one tribe might be a hindrance in doing an investigation involving the community of another tribe, but our East Africa scholar and missions veteran can quickly acquaint us with the implications. The U.S. or British embassy might brief us on the structure of the Bombay police, but the woman who ran a Christian orphanage in Bombay for thirty years and who has just taken a teaching post at a university in Michigan may know a lot more about who actually gets things done within the Bombay chain of command.

Thus in the work of seeking justice, there is a tremendous role to play for all Christians in missions, academia, international service, global business and other vocations wherein expertise in multiple countries and cultures is acquired. These experts simply need to recognize the value of their wisdom, knowledge and experience and share it with those who are pursuing interventions on behalf of the oppressed. Obviously the International Justice Mission is most grateful to add such expertise to its councils of international consultants.

Public Justice Professionals

As one might expect, there is also a critical role to play for public justice professionals who have a capacity to work in a crosscultural setting. The first task in seeking justice for the oppressed is to overcome the deception behind which oppressors hide their coercion and abuse. Accordingly, those who are professionally trained in ferreting out the facts have a critical contribution to make in defending those who are victimized by the abuse of power. Professional criminal investigators with crosscultural skills can conduct undercover investigations and other evidence-gathering operations to get proof of the abuse. They can develop detailed evidence about the nature of the abuse, the victims and the perpetrators. They can also facilitate, train and equip indigenous investigative resources that can respond to cases of oppression in the community.

Perhaps we are not accustomed to thinking about law-enforcement professionals and criminal investigators using their skills in Christian ministry. If so, we very much need to rethink such a view. If we are called to seek justice as part of building the kingdom of God, then we need to make full use of the gifts of those who possess the skills and experience to deal with coercion and deception.

Our director of investigations joined the International Justice Mission at the peak of his career as a senior-level criminal investigator. He served his community in the United States as a sheriff's detective, investigating murders, rapes, child abuse, drug trafficking and all other major felonies. He went on to head the investigative division of his law-enforcement agency, lead the SWAT team and serve as a commander with the international police task force in Bosnia, where law-enforcement officers from nearly forty countries served under his command, investigating human-rights abuses. God has equipped him in a very special way for dealing with the coercion and deception of those who abuse their power. Now on the basis of referrals from Christian ministries around the world, he identifies the police who are assaulting and extorting money from street children. He rescues girls held in forced prostitution. He brings to justice those who hold children in bonded servitude. In a given case his colleagues in the field might include a lawyer, a retired Secret Service agent or a law-enforcement officer serving on a short-term mission with the organization. He may consult by e-mail with Christian medical forensics experts or call on the expertise of a Christian judge or magistrate. All of these Christians bring extraordinary gifts to the godly task of seeking justice and rescuing the oppressed.

Christians working in government law-making bodies, foreign service, the United Nations, the military, the diplomatic core, international human-rights agencies—all may be called on to render assistance from the skills, experience and relationships that God has given them.

At the International Justice Mission, Christian public justice professionals with top-level technical skills and crosscultural capabilities have proven that they can be used of God in miraculous ways to work with indigenous communities to protect those vulnerable to abuse. Undoubtedly, this ministry requires an extraordinary combination of gifts. The sensitivity and serious risks associated with work in these contexts requires an uncompromising standard of professional excellence and technical skill. The circumstances afford no generosity for those who bring only good intentions, the best of motives or the most tender of hearts. Without a fierce commitment to the sharpest standards in operational and tactical excellence, we do not honor God or those whom we serve. But such professional excellence *must* be ruled by the fruit of the Spirit. The ministry of public justice professionals within the International Justice Mission requires, first and foremost, great spiritual resources of faith, courage, humility and a self-effacing and sacrificial spirit of service. It requires a capacity to work with meekness, love and honesty among people of other cultures, a heart that listens first and speaks last. It requires discretion, wisdom and a special measure of self-mastery and self-denial. Ultimately, it depends on a life of urgent, unceasing prayer.

But God has, in his mercy and mystery, equipped the body of Christ with men and women uniquely skilled to bear a witness for justice and to overcome deception and coercion. The body now must deploy what God has given in defense of those who are vulnerable in our world.

International Business People and Professionals

God's deployment of his ministers around the world also includes large numbers of Christian business people and professionals who have developed extensive expertise and influential relationships within the countries where they work. There are occasions when this wisdom and these relationships can not only be leveraged for successful business development but also be used in service to those who are weakest in the society. Occasionally, business executives and professionals can make direct inquiries of government authorities and business partners about specific cases of alleged abuse that come to their attention. When done respectfully, with humility and with accurate, specific facts, such inquiries can have a dramatic effect on local authorities or elites who might not otherwise have such matters brought to their attention—primarily because the victims are *very* far outside the social and economic circles in which such leaders move.

Christian business executives and professionals can seek out personal relationships with members of the indigenous church community in the country where they are working. Better still, like Christ they might seek out relationships with indigenous Christians outside the socioeconomic circles which their business relationships would otherwise have them move. Through personal relationships with the indigenous Christian community, business people working abroad can bring a Christlike sensitivity to the influence of corporate power in that community—an appreciation for the economic opportunity that can come from international investment, as well as an appreciation for the negative consequences that otherwise might go unnoticed in the formation of corporate business strategy.

In addition, international business executives and professionals may be able to open the door for tactical interventions on behalf of the victims of abuse. For example, once the International Justice Mission has performed a thoroughly factual investigation, Christian business people can provide us with a personal introduction to senior government leaders or business elites who might be able to facilitate relief for the victim. Many times we can find powerful people in the country's senior business and government circles who are eager to help when the issue is presented to them with discretion, respect and accuracy. Christians working globally as business executives and professionals are frequently in a position to access these relationships on behalf of those who are weak. These relationships can be critical in lending status and power to the cause of the vulnerable.

Finally, international business executives and professionals are also frequently in the position to provide financial support to undergird the work of seeking justice. Obviously, although the poor are frequently in need of the protections of public justice professionals, they gener-

ally cannot pay to retain such services. Even when local or international professionals may be willing to provide such services, their
livelihood, expenses and coordination must be paid for. Thus business
executives and professionals have the capacity to participate directly
in God's work of seeking justice by making it financially possible for
public justice professionals to provide these specialized services to
those who cannot pay for them. Therefore those whom God has
prospered in their international business dealings can render back to
God something of his graciousness by supporting Christian efforts to
seek justice for victims of oppression in the very nation where God
has granted successful business endeavors. There may be instances in
which the rendering of such support might be the very reason God has
granted special prosperity to a member of the worldwide Christian
family. What joy God has poured out on those who bring rescue to the
hurting in this way!

The Storytellers and Communicators

In the work of seeking justice there are two stories that deserve to be
told with passion and excellence: the stories of the victims of abuse
and the stories of what God has done to bring rescue. The boy sold
into bonded servitude, the girl held in prostitution, the student tortured
by soldiers, the widow pushed off her land—they all deserve to have
their stories told with honesty, authenticity, power and life. The
writers, producers, artists and media professionals in our Christian
community can play a vital role in bringing deliverance to the oppressed by telling their stories with all the conviction, clarity and
vividness for which they were granted their special gifts of communication. And where God in his mercy and power has brought rescue,
the story of his faithfulness needs to be told—with every tool of
communication and artistic expression at our disposal. Such stories
inspire hope, encourage the afflicted and give witness to God's glory.

An enormously profound and challenging exploration of God's

character of justice has yet to burst forth in the Christian community. What great Christian filmmakers will share with the world the epic stories of what God has done through the lives of our greatest champions of justice—the likes of Wilberforce, Sojourner Truth or Dr. Katherine Bushnell? What Christians will write the great literature of this generation as it explores the "more important matters of the law," the biblical allegories of oppression and rescue or the deep inner mysteries of power, authority, courage and deliverance? Who will write the music and render the visions that strengthen and inspire a new generation of Christian servants in the ministry of justice in a hurting world? I believe that there are great storehouses of godly creative power waiting to be poured out of those who offer themselves as vessels of the Spirit on behalf of "the least of these."

What Every Christian Can Do: Go, Send or Pray

In fact, God in his graciousness has provided a role for every Christian in his work of seeking justice. For every follower of Jesus Christ, securing rescue for the oppressed is meant to be an integral part of our life of Christian devotion simply because it is how we share in the fullness of the character of God. What a joy, what a privilege to be used of God to transform the lives of those broken by the crushing abuse of power! What poverty, what sadness, what regret to have *never* known the profound joy and satisfaction in being used of God to redeem a life from oppression and violence.

When it comes to the biblical work of seeking justice, every thoughtful and compassionate Christian can know the exhilaration, significance and challenge of being the instrument of our almighty God. Each of us can go, send or pray.

We can go where we are needed. Some of us, especially the public justice professionals discussed earlier, can go—we can make our specialized skills available to the kingdom of God throughout the world. Through the International Justice Mission such professionals travel to different countries either as full-time staff, contractors or volunteers. They carry out the investigations, interventions, training and coordination that allow the body of Christ to respond biblically to cases of abuse and oppression in the community.

We can send people who can help. Behind every professional who goes there stands a small army of faithful Christians that sends. They make it possible for some of us to minister on a full-time basis to the needs of those who are too weak to defend themselves. These supporters contribute toward the costs of project expenses and see to it that poverty doesn't preclude people from receiving justice when they need it. Every time an International Justice Mission staff member participates in rescuing a child from forced prostitution or calls to account police who have been abusing street children, they are *only* able to do so because there are scores of faithful Christians behind them.

Not everyone can travel across the world and attend to the needs of those who are hurting around the globe, but they can—they must—send people in Jesus' name. And though these faithful Christians remain at home, they play an active part in such ministries: they embolden the workers with prayers, share their burdens, offer them personal encouragement and devotion, and sustain them financially in their ministry. For many Christian business people and professionals, one of the greatest joys of their life is seeing the way God uses their resources through the work of other Christians in bringing real rescue to children brutalized by the abuse of power.

We can pray for those in the position to do what is necessary. Finally, for those who can neither go nor directly send others, there remains the most divine portion of the work—intercessory prayer. Every Christian, young or old, rich or poor, eaucated or uneducated, can bring before the Father the urgent needs of a prisoner illegally detained, the numbing despair of a child held in prostitution, the wounds of a torture victim or the suffocating burdens of a child held in bonded servitude.

The International Justice Mission has a vast network of prayer partners who, on a daily basis, take such concerns to the throne of our heavenly Father. They experience the glory of stepping into the very heart of what the Creator of the universe is doing in history. They participate in the divine redemption of the orphan and the widow as God rescues their lives from the pit. Over time, these partners come to know and love our staff members, and they uphold us and our families in prayer. They come to know the victims of abuse in tiny villages or megacities, and they challenge God to manifest his character of compassion and justice. They come to know God. They see his faithfulness, his loving kindness, his mysterious ways. In this way *every* Christian who loves Jesus can proclaim his character of love and justice around the world.

What an enormous difference we could make—what a witness we could be—if even a fraction of the Christian community in the Western world took up in earnest the ministry of seeking biblical justice in the world. If even one in ten Christians, for example, asked God where he might use them—to go, to send, to pray—there would be a witness of justice in the world that history has only yet yearned to see. Of course, as with every miracle God has prepared for his earth, he waits only for you and me to turn our hearts toward Jesus—to persevere in one holy devotion as we offer ourselves to him: "Here I am, Lord Send me."

Notes

Preface

[1]C. S. Lewis, *The Screwtape Letters*, rev. ed. (New York: Collier, 1982), pp. 137-38.

Chapter 2: Preparing the Mind & Spirit Through Scripture

[1]"World Scene: News Briefs," *Christianity Today*, June 16, 1997, p. 68.

[2]U.S. State Department, "Brazil Country Report on Human Rights Practices for 1997," January 30, 1998, http://www.state.gov/www/global/human_rights/1997_hrp_report/brazil.html

[3]U.S. State Department, "Kenya Country Report on Human Rights Practice for 1997," January 30, 1998, p. 1, http://www.state.gov/www/global/human_rights/1997_hrp_report/brazil.html

[4]U.S. State Department, "Turkey Country Report on Human Rights Practice for 1997," January 30, 1998, p. 2, http://www.state.gov/www/global/human_rights/1997_hrp_report/turkey.html

Chapter 3: Champions of Justice

[1]C. S. Lewis, *The Screwtape Letters*, rev. ed. (New York: Collier, 1982), p. 138.

[2]Dana Hardwick, *Oh Thou Woman That Bringest Good Tidings: The Life and Work of Katherine C. Bushnell* (St. Paul: Christians for Biblical Equality, 1995), p. 27.

[3]Ibid., pp. 30-31.

[4]Ibid., p. 32.

[5]Irene Ashby-MacFadyen, "Child Life vs. Dividends," *The American Federationist*, May 1902, p. 215.

[6]Hugh Bailey, *Edgar Gardner Murphy: Gentle Progressive* (Coral Gables, Fla.: University of Miami Press, 1968), p. 83.

[7]Ibid., pp. 85, 88.

[8]Ibid., p. 108.

[9]NAACP advertisement in the *New York Times*, November 1922, cited in *Who Built America*, ed. Roy Rosenzweig (New York: Pantheon, 1992), 2:303.

[10]Jessie Daniel Ames, *Southern Women and Lynching* (Atlanta: n.p., 1936), cited in Harvard Sitkoff, *A New Deal for Blacks* (New York: Oxford University Press, 1978), p. 274. An important precursor to the ASWPL in exposing the horror and injustice of lynching was the Southern Committee on the Study of Lynching (S.C.S.L.), which counted among its leaders W. J. McGlothin, president of the Southern Baptist Convention (Sitkoff, *New Deal for Blacks*, p. 271).

[11]Jessie Daniel Ames, "Reminiscences of Jessie Daniel Ames: 'I Really Do Like a Good Fight,' " interview by Pat Watters, *New South* 27 (spring 1972): 35.

[12]Sitkoff, *New Deal for Blacks*, p. 275.

[13]C. Van Woodward, *The Strange Career of Jim Crow* (New York: Oxford University Press, 1974), p. 143. Lynching did return on a diminished scale during the tensions of the civil rights movement of the 1960s.

[14]Jacquelyn Dowd Hall, *Revolt Against Chivalry: Jessie Daniel Ames and the Women's Campaign Against Lynching* (New York: Columbia University Press, 1979), p. 163.

[15]Dr. Martin Luther King Jr., commencement address to Springfield College, Springfield, Mass., June 14, 1964, http://mind.spfldcol.edu/homepage.nsf/5e02ee2e288da22385256393005bbc7a/494f5e84b19bf4d3852564bf005def28?OpenDocument.

[16]David Bosch, *Transforming Mission* (Maryknoll, N.Y.: Orbis, 1996), p. 426.

[17]Ibid., p. 510.

[18]Ibid., 508.

[19]John Gregg Fee, *Autobiography* (Chicago: n.p., 1891), cited in Sydney E. Alhstrom, *A Religious History of the American People* (New Haven, Conn.: Yale University Press, 1972), p. 653.

[20]Alhstrom, *Religious History,* pp. 637-40.

[21]Bosch, *Transforming Mission,* p. 509.

[22]Carl F. H. Henry, "A Summons to Justice," *Christianity Today,* July 20, 1992, p. 40.

Chapter 4: Hope in the God of Justice

[1]Katherine C. Bushnell, *God's Word to Women: 100 Bible Studies on Women's Place in the Divine Economy,* 2nd ed. (Oakland, Ca.: K. C. Bushnell, 1930), paragraph 13.

[2] "Caste-Related Massacre Claims Sixty-one Lives in India," *Washington Post,* December 3, 1997, p. A38.

Chapter 5: Hope in the God of Compassion

[1]Some may be troubled by the theological notion of an all-sufficient God who suffers, but like the Reverend John Stott, I believe it is inherent in God's willful commitment to love: "The best way to confront the traditional view of the impassibility of God [i.e., the notion that God is incapable of suffering], however, is to ask 'what meaning can there be in a love which is not costly to a lover.' If love is self giving, then it is inevitably vulnerable to pain, since it exposes itself to the possibility of rejection and insult. 'It is the fundamental Christian assertion that God is love,' writes Jürgen Moltmann, 'which in principle broke the Aristotelian doctrine of God' (as 'impassible'). 'Were God incapable of suffering . . . then he would also be incapable of love,' whereas 'the one who is capable of love is also capable of suffering, for he also opens himself up to the suffering which is involved in love.' That is surely why Bonhoeffer wrote from prison to his friend Eberhard Bethge, nine months before his execution: 'only the Suffering God can help.' " John Stott, *The Cross of Christ* (Downers Grove, Ill.: InterVarsity Press, 1986), p. 332.

Chapter 6: Hope in the God of Moral Clarity

[1]J. I. Packer, *Knowing God* (Downers Grove, Ill.: InterVarsity Press, 1973), p. 144.

[2]Ibid., p. 142.

[3]Ibid., p. 136.

[4]Ibid., p. 128.

[5]Dietrich Bonhoeffer, *Letters and Papers from Prison* (New York: Macmillan, 1972), pp. 4-5.

[6]Dietrich Bonhoeffer, "Who Stands Fast?" in *The Martyred Christian: 160 Readings from Dietrich Bonhoeffer* (New York: Collier, 1983), p. 157.

Chapter 8: Answers for Difficult Questions

[1]Richard Cohen, "Savagery in Algeria," *Washington Post,* January 15, 1998, A23.

[2]Feodor Dostoyevsky, *The Brothers Karamazov* (New York: Bantam, 1981), p. 286.

[3]C. S. Lewis, *The Problem of Pain* (New York: Collier, 1962), p. 69.

[4]Irving Greenberg, quoted in David P. Gushee, *The Righteous Gentiles of the Holocaust* (Minneapolis: Fortress, 1994), p. xii.

[5]Salvian, *The Governance of God,* in Fathers of the Church, ed. Harold Dressler (Washington, D.C.: The Catholic University of America Press, 1947), p.3.

[6]John Stott, *The Cross of Christ* (Downers Grove, Ill.: InterVarsity Press, 1986), p. 335-36.

[7]The phrase "intolerable compliment" is from Lewis, *Problem of Pain,* p. 42; "terrible gift of freedom" is from Dostoyevsky, *Brothers Karamazov,* p. 309.

[8]Dostoyevsky, *Brothers Karamazov,* p. 308.

[9]Lewis, *Problem of Pain,* 144.

[10]Matthew Bridges and Godfrey Thring, "Crown Him with Many Crowns."

Chapter 9: Anatomy of Injustice

[1]G. K. Chesterton, *What's Wrong with the World* (San Francisco: Ignatius Press, 1994), chap. 5.

[2]Samson Gahungu, "Letter from Burundi," *The Friend,* April 19, 1996, p. 21.

[3]Samson Gahungu, "Letter from Burundi," *The Friend,* January 17, 1997, p. 11.

[4]Ibid.

[5]When Saul persecuted the church, he based it "on the authority of the chief priests" and "tried to force them to blaspheme" so he would have legal authority to throw them in prison (Acts 26:10-11).

[6]*Manila Times,* February 11, 1989, quoted in *Impunity: Prosecutions of Human Rights Violations in the Philippines* (New York: Lawyers Committee for Human Rights, 1991), p. 31.

[7]"Provost Marshal General Report to Chief of Staff of AFP," quoted in *Impunity,* p. 51.

[8]*Manila Chronicle,* July 14, 1989, quoted in *Impunity,* p. 127.

[9]*Manila Journal,* July 14, 1989, quoted in *Impunity,* p. 126.

[10]Ibid.

Chapter 11: Intervening for the Victims

[1]The South African story is clearly more complicated than this; it was a struggle strewn with the corpses and casualties of violent white resistance to change. The international sanctions and the violent pressures of the black political struggle definitely had an impact. But had the white South Africans had the *will* to use all the force at their disposal and to endure the relatively mild consequences of international sanctions, they certainly would have had the power to maintain their apartheid way of life well into the twenty-first century. The power of personal appeals to spiritual convictions, morality, and notions of common human decency is beautifully chronicled in Michael Cassidy's *A Witness Forever* (London: Hodder & Stoughton, 1995).

[2]There are exceptions, of course. It was a U.N.-sponsored force that recently threw a horrible military clique out of power in Sierra Leone. It is the U.N. that is bringing the perpetrators of genocidal crimes in Rwanda and Bosnia to justice. And it is under the U.N. umbrella that Saddam Hussein is being restricted in his ambitions to deploy weapons of mass destruction.

[3]U.S. Department of State, "Nigeria Country Report on Human Rights Practices for 1997," January 30, 1998, pp. 1-2, http://www.state.gov/www/global/human_rights/1997_hrp_report/nigeria.html
[4]Human Rights Committee, Comments on Nigeria, U.N. Doc. CCPR/C/79/Add.65 (1996).
[5]Human Rights Watch, "Human Rights Watch Africa," http://www.hrw.org/hrw/about/divisions/africa.html

Chapter 12: The Body of Christ in Action

[1]Of course, the exportation of Western cultural baggage does continue to some extent; but when it does, it happens contrary to the missionary's own best theory and training. Missionaries rightly believe in the power of the gospel to *transform* the cultural (as in mitigating cultural traditions of headhunting or bride burning), the way Christians in America believe that the gospel should be a force of transformation within their own culture of materialism, arrogance, hedonism, etc. But most international Christian workers have traveled light-years in understanding the difference between exporting the idiosyncrasies of their own cultures and allowing the transcendent verities of the gospel affect each community in its own indigenous culture.

Additional Resources for Study & Reflection

World Vision and the International Justice Mission have cooperated with InterVarsity Press to develop outstanding resources to accompany *Good News About Injustice*. This study guide and video are ideally suited for use by small groups, adult education classes, mission committees and college courses to enhance understanding of God's response to situations of injustice and ways God is calling Christians to respond.

Good News About Injustice study guide: A four-week study that focuses on how God empowers his people to join in his work on behalf of the oppressed. This discussion-oriented study integrates reflections on portions of *Good News About Injustice* with opportunities to analyze biblical texts. Illustrated by both the companion video and stories from around the world, this study enables groups of address some of the tough questions raised by injustice and what we can do about it. *Order #2235, $4.99*

Good News About Injustice video: Designed as a companion to the study guide, the forty minute video features former president Jimmy Carter sharing his passion, insight and work on behalf of the poor and oppressed. The video also portrays contemporary situations of grave injustice such as forced prostitution, child labor, child soldiers and other gripping issues. Each video segment is designed to accompany one week of the four-week study guide, allowing participants to enter into the lives of people around the world. *Length: approximately 40 minutes, order #2236, $14.99*

These resources may be ordered from your local bookstore or from any of the following:

World Vision
P.O. Box 9716
Federal Way, WA 98063-9716
1-888-511-6484

International Justice Mission
P.O. Box 58147
Washington, DC 20037-8147

InterVarsity Press
P.O. Box 1400
Downers Grove, IL 60515

For more information about how
you can be involved in God's work
of justice, contact the
International Justice Mission:

P.O. Box 58147
Washington, D.C. 20037-8147

Phone: 703.536.3730
Fax: 703.536.3790
Email: ijm@ix.netcom.com
Website· www.ijm.org